# ANTIGUA
### AND
# BARBUDA

## A LITTLE BIT OF PARADISE

**HANSIB**

# ANTIGUA
## AND
# BARBUDA
## A LITTLE BIT OF PARADISE

*Edited by Arif Ali*

**HANSIB**

First published in Great Britain 1988
by Hansib Publications Ltd
Second edition published in 1994
Third edition published in 1996

This edition published in 1999
by Hansib Publications Ltd
Tower House, 141-149 Fonthill Road,
London N4 3HF, England

© Hansib Publications Ltd
Photographs © Nicole Mouck

A catalogue record of this book is
available from the British Library

ISBN 1 870518 57 8

Design & Production by Graphic Resolutions, Welwyn
Colour Origination by Graphic Ideas Studios, London
Printed and bound in Britain by Caledonian
International Book Manufacturing Ltd, Glasgow

# ACKNOWLEDGEMENTS

Text by Ronald M Sanders CMG, MA

Photographs by Nicole Mouck

Prime Minister of Antigua and Barbuda, Lester Bird who, when Deputy Prime Minister and Tourism Minister, commissioned the first edition of Antigua and Barbuda: A Little Bit of Paradise, published in 1988, and who has continued to support all further editions; Antigua and Barbuda Minister of Tourism, Rodney Williams and his team; Chief of Staff in the Office of the Prime Minister, Asot Michael; Antigua and Barbuda High Commissioner in London, His Excellency Ronald M Sanders and his entire staff; Photographer, Allan Aflak who provided all the photographs for the previous three editions of 'A Little Bit of Paradise' and with whom the publication will always be associated; Antigua and Barbuda Senators, Henderson Simon, Kenrick Isaac and Max Fernandez; Rob Barratt and all the staff at the Royal Antiguan Resort; Azez Hadeed; Moti Persaud; Leone Yorke; Sheila Fenton; Myrna Lake; Beverley Bernard; Joyce Edwards; Peter Nurse; Gaston Browne; Lolita and Antoine Aflak; Photographer, Timothy Payne of the Antigua Sun newspaper; Jackal Photo Studio; Photographer, Ashley Hanley of Photogenesis; Louis Daniel of the Antigua Sun newspaper; John Bird and the staff at BWIA in London; Vino Patel of Flight Connections; Dr Babu; Lorna Simon; and Martin Robertson, who sadly passed away in 1998, and who will always be remembered for his sterling support and, above all, for his dear friendship for many years.

Arif Ali
January 1999

# THE NATIONAL COAT OF ARMS

The Pineapple on top of the heraldic helmet represents the famous Antigua black pineapple. The Red Hibiscus flowers are symbolic of the many varieties of this plant found in abundance on the islands. The Shield with the Golden Sun and wavy blue and white bands of the National Flag symbolises the sun, sea and beaches for which Antigua and Barbuda are renowned. The Old Sugar Mill and the stem of sugar cane have historical roots and depict the cultivation of sugar cane for the production of sugar, which was Antigua's main industry. The Yucca plant or 'Spanish bayonet', with its upright stem and showy edible flower cluster at its summit was the old emblem of Antigua. The deer are symbolic of the wild-life that inhabited pre-colonial Antigua and Barbuda. The scroll bears the motto of the nation, "Each endeavouring, all achieving."

## THE DESIGNER OF THE COAT OF ARMS

The National Coat of Arms was designed by Gordon Christopher with a little modification by the Statehood Celebrations Committee, 1966. Mr Christopher was born in Antigua and emigrated to Canada in 1967. In 1971, he gained a diploma in Applied Art at the Alberta College of Art, and in 1974 he graduated from the University of Calgary with a Bachelor of Fine Arts Degree. Since then, he has been an active painter, printmaker, graphic designer and instructor in art. His work has been exhibited nationally and internationally and is included in both private and public collections in Canada and the United States. He is a member of the Alberta Society of Artists.

# THE MOTTO OF THE NATION

The motto of the nation is, "Each endeavouring, all achieving." It was composed by James H Carrott MBE in 1967 when he was Permanent Secretary in the Ministry of Trade, Production and Labour. According to Mr Carrott, "The concept was to provide inspiration to each Antiguan and Barbudan to recognise that the development of the whole country would be a benefit to all, but that development required the effort of each individual."

## THE NATIONAL FLAG

The golden sun image symbolises the
dawn of a new era; red symbolises the
dynamism of the people; blue
represents hope; black symbolises the
soil and the nation's African heritage;
gold, blue and white represent
Antigua's natural tourist attractions -
sun, sea and sand; and the 'v' shape
symbolises 'victory'.

### DESIGNER OF THE FLAG

The flag of Antigua and Barbuda was designed in 1967 when the country became a State in Association with
Britain. Its designer, Reginald Samuel, is an Antiguan artist, sculptor, painter and art teacher. His design was
selected from among 600 entries.

## THE NATIONAL ANTHEM

Words by Novelle H Richards, music
by Walter P Chambers, arrangement
by H A Kenney

# Contents

# CHAPTER ONE

# Morning has broken

The sun, like a huge, ripe orange, rises slowly from behind the Caribbean sea. Streaks of light - some yellow, some red, yet others brightly white - strike out across the water, dancing on the peaks of gentle, little waves as they meander towards a shore still cast in night's receding shadow, but already exposing beaches of white and golden sands. It is daybreak in Antigua and Barbuda... and everyday is summer.

As the sun ascends - boldly now, for, like the day, it too is fully awake - its golden glow begins to disappear, yielding to a stunning brightness which hurls itself across the sea and onto the land. The atmosphere is still cool, for even though the sun has begun to proclaim its dominion over the earth, its heat is still young and unable to penetrate the cool, north-east Trade Winds which blow steadily across the sea.

In an age old tradition, tiny fishing boats oscillate on the sea, making their way back to the shore, laden with fish for the morning's market. The fishermen set sail during the night knowing that daybreak would lure fish to the sea's surface in ritual welcome to the radiance of a newborn sun before its heat forced them to seek cooler waters near the ocean floor. The rhythmic chug of the fishing boats' small, outboard engines mixes with the louder roar of bigger engines on jet-skis, motor boats and yachts as those who cater for visitors begin to prepare their equipment for the day's coterie of people anxious to make the most of a Caribbean holiday.

Slowly now, people begin to appear: first, young natives of Antigua and Barbuda - their bodies bristling with health, their muscles well developed - jogging along the beach and occasionally diving into the water to be refreshed by its invigorating sting. Visitors too come in this early morning light and, with a sense of longing at last fulfilled, immerse themselves into the sea, stretching out on their backs, relaxing their muscles, letting tensions dissipate, their faces raised to catch the tingling touch of the sun's glorious rays.

Birds too are part of the morning's activity. There are 140 species on Antigua and Barbuda, 90 of which are seen regularly. Some are hunters - such as the brown pelicans skimming along the sea, suddenly plunging into the water only to rise again abruptly, their morning meal caught in their beaks. Others flit from tree to tree calling out in song and adding to the ambience of nature in all its perfection. The bananaquit and the lesser Antillean bullfinch, black or grey with a reddish breast are the most common.

As the sun gains in ascendancy, bathing the land in light, colours come alive - leaves are now vivid green, flowers - the exotic bougainvillaea, the hibiscus and the oleander - are red, yellow, white and even purple.

Coconut trees and other palms, that have stood majestically on the shores of these islands for decades, climb upwards toward the clear blue sky dotted only here and there with soft, white clouds. Occasionally either a very old or a very young palm, responding to pressure from the wind, arches downwards - but even this curve has a certain grace, an attractiveness that speaks not of submission to an unwelcome force, but of surrender to the allure of nature.

The shores - 365 beaches and coves - are the beginnings of "a little bit of paradise", the same paradise that Christopher Columbus encountered on 11 November 1493 when on his second journey to what he called the 'new world', he saw the islands and, without setting foot on them, named one 'Barbuda', and the other 'Antigua' after the church of Santa Maria de la Antigua in Seville, Spain.

*Sunset over the Atlantic Ocean*

*Heavily laden coconut palm*

*Natural rock formation known locally as Devil's Bridge*

*Brightly coloured dwarf poinciana*

*Allamander, or golden trumpet*

*Footprints in the sand at Galley Bay*

*Frigate birds in Barbuda's bird sanctuary*

*A beach for every day of the week*

*Sunset over Hudson Point*

# CHAPTER TWO

# *Paradise presented*

Welcome to paradise - pearls of natural beauty set in the jewel of the blue Caribbean Sea! Before we unfold the drama of the settlement, colonisation and evolution of these islands, we should survey the scene of the activity.

The territory of Antigua and Barbuda actually consists of three main islands Antigua, Barbuda and Redonda although there are several small dependent islands around Antigua such as Guiana Island, Bird Island and Long Island. Antigua is 108 square miles (280 sq km), Barbuda is 62 sq miles (160 sq km) and Redonda is 0.6 sq miles (1.6 sq km).

Redonda is uninhabited and there are approximately 70,000 people on Antigua and 1,200 on Barbuda. The last population census was done in 1991. When the previous census was conducted in the 1980s, Antigua's population was 78,000 and Barbuda's 1,500. This decline in population is due to the emigration of native Antiguans and Barbudans. Since the 1930s, many families have ensured that at least one child is born in the United States of America, allowing for other family members to emigrate there - pursuing a different kind of paradise.

Ninety-one percent of the people of Antigua and Barbuda are of African descent. Their forefathers were brought as slaves in the 17th and 18th centuries from the West Coast of Africa. The rest of the population is made up of Lebanese and Syrians who came as traders at the beginning of this century; the descendants of Portuguese - 2,500 of whom came as labourers from Madeira between 1847, when a famine plagued that island, and 1852; Americans, Canadians and Europeans who settled during this century and West Indians mainly from Dominica, Montserrat, St Kitts and Guyana. Recently, there has been a small influx of Chinese from the Peoples Republic of China who entered the country as workers in the small garment industry. Some have since opened modest Chinese restaurants.

The political structure of the country is firmly rooted in parliamentary democracy patterned on the system in Britain. There are several political parties which contest elections at least every five years when Antiguans and Barbudans of 18 and over can vote to choose a government. The country is divided into 17 constituencies and parties contesting the elections nominate one candidate for election in each constituency. A general election is won by the party whose candidates are elected in nine or more constituencies. The victorious party then forms a government consisting of a Prime Minister and several Ministers.

*Jolly Beach and Club Antigua*

The State system comprises the government, parliament, the judiciary and the Head of State.

Antigua and Barbuda's Head of State is Queen Elizabeth II who is also Head of State in Britain and several other Commonwealth countries. The Queen is represented in Antigua and Barbuda by a Governor-General selected by the Government. The role of the Head of State is largely ceremonial although the Constitution of the country vests certain limited powers in the office.

Parliament has two chambers - an assembly of representatives of parties or individuals who are elected by the majority votes in the constituencies, and a Senate whose members are appointed by the Governor-General, the Prime Minister and the leader of the opposition in parliament. Parliament makes the laws of the country.

The Judiciary is entirely independent of the government. Both judges and appeal court judges are appointed by the consensus of seven governments in the Eastern Caribbean. This makes it difficult for individual governments to attempt to influence the Court against its own judgement of the law.

This is the scene of paradise on which our story begins...

*Curtain Bluff Hotel*

*Panoramic view of Dickenson Bay from the hillside above the Rex Halcyon Cove Hotel*

*White and pink sand, and
turquoise waters extend for miles
along Palm Beach on Barbuda*

*Club Antigua at Jolly Beach*

*Galley Bay Resort*

*A tour boat approaches Luis Beach on Barbuda*

# CHAPTER THREE

# *Paradise found*

The islands of Antigua and Barbuda are a banquet of beauty; a feast of sunshine, sand and sea to delight the most discriminating gourmet. With over 365 beaches, the twin-islands offer a regimen of water-sports, deep-sea diving, reef exploration, yachting, plentiful fishing and lazy bathing that is without comparison anywhere in the world.

The beaches range from dazzling white to golden sands; the water is warm, gentle and crystal clear. No experience quite matches slumbering on a beach chair, under a coconut tree at sundown as the water softly laps against the shore while the sound of a distant steelband wafts through the air. Paradise indeed; after the dark and chill of European and North American winters.

For centuries this paradise remained unknown to most Europeans and North Americans except for the traveller fascinated by the West Indies. While none of these wanderers failed to endorse the beauty of the islands, it was not until 1949 that the paradise of Antigua was found by a group of millionaires who successfully kept it secret for many years.

This millionaire group with holiday homes in Bermuda sought another more exclusive and remote location for their winter frolics. After much investigation,

they decided upon Antigua and set up the Mill Reef Club in 1949. The early membership was impressive and included Paul Mellon and his wife (Exxon Oil), Laurens Hammond (Hammond Organ), Philip Reed former Chairman of General Electric and Henry Ketch the inventor of the cartoon character 'Dennis the Menace'. They constructed an exclusive estate with million dollar homes and private beaches, a common clubhouse, a 9 hole golf course and tennis courts.

Mill Reef Club continues in Antigua as it always has - unintrusively and imperceptibly. While it creates no offence to the Antiguans, the Club and individual members - the Mellons particularly - have been helpful to the community by providing scholarships for University education and contributing to worthy causes such as facilities at the Holberton Hospital, a public institution.

When the United States imposed its blockade on Cuba in 1960 after the rise of Fidel Castro, Americans began to look around for other holiday islands in the Caribbean. Many of them, following the lead of the Mill Reefers, found Antigua and started visiting in increasing numbers.

It is small wonder that in the early 1960s, the government of Antigua and

Barbuda took advantage of the islands' natural attractions to promote tourism. From very modest beginnings, the tourist industry is now the most important sector of the economy, contributing 80 per cent to the Gross Domestic Product (GDP).

The country boasts 40 hotels and 21 guest houses and apartments with 140 restaurants offering sumptuous cuisine that spreads from exotic local dishes to Italian, French and Swiss-German fayre. Nightclubs and discotheques have mushroomed providing a variety of entertainment but especially the rhythms of calypso and the scintillating beat of the steel band.

Casinos are also available to the tourists who would like to live a little dangerously.

Tourism directly employs 35 per cent of the nation's workforce. Taxi-drivers, workers in boutiques and other shops, handicraft makers and sellers - all of these also benefit from tourism.

Aside from the beaches, the country offers spectacular sailing. Few pleasures match the sailors delight in leisurely meandering through the blue Caribbean waters sailing to secluded coves and sheltered beaches for a day of quiet bliss. Those who like a "jump up" on the sea, favour cruising on the "Jolly Roger", a converted pirate ship, which provides all the booze anyone can drink with good food and music, while it sails the waters off Antigua. Those, who prefer exploring the world beneath the sea, are enchanted by the coral reefs and multi-coloured fish that characterise Antiguan and Barbudan waters.

Sports enthusiasts quickly discover the lawn tennis courts and the fact that professional aspirants flock to Antigua for "Tennis Week" in January to test their skills against each other and to train for the international circuit. Golf fans are delighted with the 18 hole golf courses at Cedar Valley and Jolly Harbour.

Tourists are visiting Antigua and Barbuda in increasing numbers. In 1976, there were 56,398 visitors, by 1992, over 144,873, and in 1998 a total of 488,897 people visited the islands. Alongside the development of facilities for the tourist and measures to increase the earnings of locals from the industry, the Government has built the modern V C Bird International Airport. The airport provides direct connections to Frankfurt, London, Miami, New York and Toronto. In addition, Antigua is the gateway to the Eastern Caribbean and South America with several flights daily to most Caribbean countries. Further, having been served for years by a deep water harbour, outside of St John's, the Government decided to construct an entirely new harbour especially for cruise ships on the very edge of the town. Now, passengers on cruise ships disembark into the heart of St John's. In a real sense the new port and Airport symbolise the significance and importance of tourism to the people of Antigua and Barbuda, for while they will serve visitors to the country, equally they will benefit locals. And that, in essence, is what tourism in Antigua and Barbuda is all about - service to the visitors and benefits for the people in an atmosphere of genuine friendliness and warmth.

There are now 3,620 rooms available for tourists in Antigua and Barbuda. These include exclusive hotels such as the magnificent Coco Point Lodge on Barbuda, the picturesque Jumby Bay on Long Island, and the all-inclusive hotel for couples, Sandals, which sits on magnificent Dickenson Bay in Antigua. The Ramada Renaissance Royal Antiguan is the country's largest hotel combining all the elements of an idyllic Caribbean holiday with superb conference facilities.

One of the largest hotel resorts in the Caribbean is Jolly Harbour Beach Resort situated on 500 acres of land including

*Barbuda's private and secluded K Club*

two fingers which extend into a harbour and man made island. The development includes a hotel, waterfront villas, a marina for 140 berths, a boat building shop, a shopping centre, restaurants, and a golf course. The aim of the developer, Alfred Erhart, was to create a sense of community between vacationers and the local population. Strolling through Jolly Harbour certainly gives the impression a sense of community has been achieved.

All beach hotels offer a variety of water sports including water ski-ing, jet ski-ing and wind surfing. Arrangements are also made for scuba diving, deep sea fishing or cruises.

*Coco Point Beach Resort, Barbuda*

'The Spirit of Antigua', operated by Wadadli Cats cruises, moored at the Antigua Yacht Club

*The marina at Falmouth Harbour*

*Parasailing is a popular attraction*

*Rex Blue Heron Hotel*

*Mango Bay Hotel is a peaceful retreat on the east coast*

*Gaugin Cottages at
the Galley Bay Resort*

*Hawksbill Beach Hotel*

*Hawksbill Beach Hotel
at Five Islands*

*Sunset Cove Hotel at Runaway Bay*

*The Jolly Roger pirate ship offers a popular and fun-filled day cruise*

*Marina Bay Hotel at Runaway Bay*

*Sandals Antigua
at Dickenson Bay*

*Accessible only by boat, Barbuda's Palm Beach stretches for miles*

# CHAPTER FOUR

# *Morning till night*

From the crack of dawn, the ever present sun reaches into every nook and cranny of house and hotel waking up sleepy eyes.

But, in the rural areas of Antigua, farmers are up before the sun to prepare a meal before heading to their land. These folk are the salt of the earth, their bodies aged but lean and strong from years of toil, they are god fearing: gentle despite their strength, mannerly and correct despite their ruggedness.

Many of them have only small subsistence plots from which, year after year, they have produced crops for sale in the market place or to the Government Marketing Corporation. Their enemies do not exist among men; their foes are pests which threaten their plants and rains which seldom come. Some of them rear cattle and, day after day, armed with a prodding stick and wearing a wide straw hat to shade their heads from the sun, they walk the land, leading a herd of goats or cows, looking for good grazing ground.

For the most part, these are older people who have worked to educate their children and, in doing so, have lost the majority of them from the land. These same children, now grown up, work in offices and hotels. They too rise before the sun to catch the buses which leave the countryside early in the morning to bring passengers to central points in St John's

from which they disperse to work. The bus ride is an animated affair - in a community so small, few are strangers and the journey is filled with excited conversation and laughter. Occasionally, there is a quarrel, but even this is a kind of theatre: seldom going beyond the point of loud voices, the body language of threat and counter threat - so naturally expressed - could have been choreographed for the stage. Fellow passengers, like any good audience, fully enjoy a spectacle they know will go no further than histrionics.

No morning is a morning to lie in bed - not even for the holiday maker. The greater luxury is to bask on the beach, enjoying the contrasting sensations of warming sunshine and cooling breeze. But first breakfast... breakfast in all combinations - American, European and West Indian: eggs and bacon, croissant and danish or salted fish. And what delicious fruits - pineapple, papaw and guava which were here before Columbus; bananas and oranges brought to the Caribbean by the Spanish; mango brought from west Africa by the British.

The ultimate luxury in life is to have breakfast against the backdrop of the Caribbean Sea - as blue as all the songs say it is - listening to waves as they amble up to the shore and gently splash across the hardened sand.

Beach activity is a dazzle of colour in a

*The main intersection in Codrington, Barbuda*

combination of busy jet skis, catamarans, yachts and billowing sails. Alongside this are vendors, mostly women - some short and buxom, others tall and thin, occasionally a few both tall and buxom. Their summons to buy their wares - colourful dresses, T-shirts, beads, costume jewellery made of local material - are friendly and challenging. The beach bar opens early doing a brisk business in fruit punches for kids and the faint of heart: doing better trade in rum punches for the brave.

The sea has distinctive attraction, best appreciated by snorkelling. The water over the reefs is crystal clear and reveal a colourful marine life with parrot fish, puffers, moray eel and trumpet fish darting this way and that. Deep sea diving, of course, provides a better view of the rich marine life under the sea. Keen fishermen will also find a variety of fish such as snapper, grouper, wahoo, kingfish and lobsters which abound in the waters between Antigua and Barbuda.

As the sun finally sets on these islands bringing another day to an end and relinquishing its hold to the night, the yachts come home to dock, the beaches give up their guests to the restaurants and nightclubs, offices and factories release their workers to nocturnal pursuits. A cool atmosphere descends upon the islands as the sun disappears beyond the sea's horizon.

It is the Caribbean moon that now claims dominion, casting a romanic light across the land and onto the waters of the Caribbean and Atlantic.

Restaurants offering a wide cuisine welcome guests to candlelight and serenading minstrels. The nightclubs start much later and carry on until the small hours of the morning. The bars serve drinks to local and visitors alike. For the adventurous, moonlight cruises on a cool Caribbean Sea are also available.

The day has been filled with activity. The night has wound it down gently and a taste has been shared of the 'little bit of paradise' that is Antigua and Barbuda.

*Monarch of the Seas at Heritage Quay*

*The terminal building of Codrington Airport, one of two airstrips on Barbuda*

*The Peoples Church
in Codrington*

*Young Barbudan school children taking a short break*

*The Barbuda Pentecostal Church in Codrington*

*The ruins of Martello Tower, Barbuda*

*Jolly Harbour resort, marina and shopping complex*

*St James's Club at Mamora Bay*

*Antigua Village Hotel at Dickenson Bay*

*Pineapple Beach Club
at Long Bay*

*The reception at St James's Club*

# CHAPTER FIVE

# *Morning before yesterday*

**M**an inhabited these islands before Christ was born. According to a group of experts:

"It may have been in the neighbourhood of ten thousand years before Christ that the first Amerindians, who we now call Paleo-Indians, navigated by primitive canoe to thread their way between Antigua and Barbuda's barrier reef to land on her white sandy beaches. Sea levels were then at least 275 feet lower than they are today so that Antigua and Barbuda were linked together."

It has been established that people of the Meso-Indian age lived on Antigua as far back as 1775 BC at Jolly Beach. They were called the 'Siboney' (stone people). While around 500 BC, nomadic wanderers lived and fished at North Sound, there were no settlements on the island until 35 AD when some Amerindians of the Arawak tribe moved from their home in Venezuela and settled near Indian Creek establishing fishing villages, some agriculture and pottery. Around 1200 AD another tribe of Amerindians, the Caribs, also came up the chain of islands from South America. They established settlements in Dominica and St Kitts from where they attacked the Arawaks on Antigua taking their women and children as slaves and murdering the men. They called Antigua, 'Waladli', Barbuda, 'Wa'omoni' and Redonda, 'Ocanamanru'.

ANTIGUA: The foundation of Antigua is a large mass of volcanic rock, occupying 40-45% of the 108 square miles (280 sq km) of the island, the rest of it is formed of sedimentary rocks, mainly limestone.

Antigua can be divided into three principal regions:

- a high region consisting of precipitous hills of volcanic formation, many over 1,000 feet high. The highest point is Boggy Peak at just over 1,300 feet;
- a rolling lowland (knows as the central plain) running from St John's, the capital city, in the north-west to the spectacular Willoughby Bay in the south-east, and occupying about 20 square miles of the island; and
- a limestone area between the hills and the plain.

Antigua's shape has been described as akin to an ink blot. Its coastline - over 90 miles long - is jagged creating hundreds of coves and bays, many with fine white sand. There are also extensive coral reefs which not only maintain magnificent marine life, but also protect the coast from erosion and provide calm waters in the bays.

The island gets very little rainfall, an average of 45 inches a year. Droughts are common place and sometimes there is no rainfall for years. This absence of rain is due in great measure to the policy of the

colonial sugar planters who wantonly cut down trees to plant sugar cane.

Previously, the island was lush and thickly wooded. It had evergreen forests of red and white cedar and whitewood. In the forests lived colourful birds including the parrot. After almost a century of forest destruction, a Governor of the Island, Thomas Shirley, was forced to record in 1781:

"By this injudicious step, the fruits of the earth are deprived of those periodical supplies of moisture from rain... four or five years of dry weather will occur scorching with heat the whole island."

BARBUDA: Barbuda is mostly a flat plain except for a small area called The Highlands which rises to a maximum of 128 feet. The entire island is a limestone formation. It gets less rainfall than Antigua and has no streams or lakes, However, its beach at Coco Point is regarded by many seasoned travellers as the most beautiful in the Caribbean. Almost the whole coastline of Barbuda is edged with coral reefs which simultaneously makes it dangerous for shipping and majestic for scuba divers.

REDONDA: The majority of Antiguans and Barbudans have never seen Redonda which has always been an 'isolated, precipitous and forbidding rocky island'. It is one mile long and less than half a mile wide rising to 1,000 feet with steep cliffs on all sides. On 10 November 1493, the day before he sailed past Antigua, Columbus by-passed the rock and, in the process, named it Santa Maria la Redonda. Over the years it has been used in a variety of transient ways, including growing cassava for seafarers on the saddle on the top of the rock, issuing postage stamps and mining phosphates from bird guano. However, it is only as a haven for birds that it remains useful.

*Cocos at Jolly Bay*

*Sea Sports Ltd on Dickenson Bay offers a wide variety of water sports*

*Late afternoon on the deck
at the Galley Bay Resort*

*Frigate Birds are the main inhabitants
of the Barbuda Bird Sanctuary*

*Turners Beach Bar and Grill is popular with locals and visitors*

*The Commissioner Grill on Lower Redcliffe Street in St John's is owned by local Antiguan Conroy White*

*The beachfront at OJ's Bar and Restaurant at Crab Hill in St Mary's*

*OJ's Bar and Restaurant at Crab Hill is rated as one of the best beach canteens in the Caribbean. It is owned and operated by Oliver Joseph, who returned home to Antigua after living abroad for many years*

*Lush tropical gardens at Siboney Beach Club on Dickenson Bay*

*Twilight at the Royal Antiguan*

# CHAPTER SIX

# *Yesterday morn'*

Antigua was first settled by Europeans in an area now called Old Road. The settlers were English and, led by Captain Edward Warner, came from England's principal West Indian colony, St Kitts. Apart from a brief period in 1666 when it was captured by the French, Antigua remained British until its independence on 1 November, 1981. Today the country continues to be a Monarchical State sharing Queen Elizabeth 11 as its Head of State with Britain and several other Commonwealth countries. Barbuda used to be a separate British possession until 1 August, 1860 when it was formally annexed to Antigua.

The man directly responsible for the link between Antigua and Barbuda was Sir Christopher Codrington who came to Antigua from Barbados in 1674 and established the first large sugar estate, which he named Betty's Hope, after his daughter. Located on the south side of the main road to Long Bay, the ruins of the estate house and a working wind mill today provide an insight into the activity on this plantation three centuries ago.

Sugar production dominated Antigua until the 1970s, utilising most of the land and leaving a legacy of grave economic problems. Previously, tobacco was the main crop produced by the settlers on Antigua.

On 6 January 1685, Codrington was also granted a lease of Barbuda from the British Crown as an annexe to his estates on Antigua. The annual fee required of him for the lease was 'one fat sheep if asked'. From Barbuda, the Codringtons supplied their Antigua holdings with timber, ground provisions, fish, livestock and draught animals for more than 200 years.

It has been suggested that Barbuda was a 'stud farm' on which the Codringtons bred 'quality slaves'. Even Barbudans themselves tended to believe this, hence the Barbuda Brotherhood Social Club of New York is reported as asserting in a 1977 publication that "Barbuda was used as the experimental breeding ground for slaves, thus producing some of the strongest people in the West Indies." However, scholarly research of this claim debunks it completely. Having studied the period and the documents related to it, two eminent scholars, David Lowenthal and Colin G Clarke record:

"There never was a deliberate program of slave breeding in Barbuda, nor did the Codringtons ever contemplate this as a possibility. At the very most they envisaged Barbuda as a "nursery" to which slave children might be brought to be fed and cared for, and later taken off to work on the Antigua estates, but not even this proposal was realized."

Apart from providing food and livestock to their Antigua plantations, Barbuda's principal benefit to the Codringtons was a base from which to salvage ships which ran aground or wrecked on the reefs off Barbuda. The profits from the salvage operations went to the Codringtons who owned the men, boats and all the "equipment available for salvage operations."

Codrington's success with sugar encouraged other planters and soon there was a proliferation of sugar estates across Antigua. By 1705 most of the island was planted and 170 mills were erected for crushing cane. The windmills replaced the earlier oxen-driven mills and output of sugar per factory more than doubled. Many of these mills can still be seen today around the island.

Accompanying the spread of sugar estates was the almost complete annihilation of vegetation. As Gregson Davis put it in 'Antigua Black', 'the evergreen woodland was levelled in a manner as thorough as it was irreversible and short-sighted'. Hence apart from the lush Fig Tree Drive, there is a lamentable absence of forests and woods in Antigua today. But the defacing of the natural beauty of the island was not the only consequence of the wanton destruction of vegetation: as noted earlier, drought was the principal result of an absence of trees to attract rainfall. The government has sought to tackle this problem by creating Potswork Dam, a huge man-made lake in the centre of Antigua, and installing desalinisation plants to convert sea water for domestic and industrial use.

By 1678, half the island's population consisted of slaves brought from the west coast of Africa to cultivate sugar. The harrowing and inhuman system of slavery is well known. The lot of the slaves in Antigua was no different from their counterparts in the Caribbean and North and South America - the Antigua slaves were whipped and worked from sun up to sun down; resistance was met with foul punishments including dismembering of the body.

Naturally, many rebelled and only musket and shot compelled them to remain captive.

Some particular events relevant to Antigua are worth recalling here. In 1789 and repeatedly until 1816, the Codrington family, who had taken up residence in Gloucester, England, wrote letters to the managers of their estates on Antigua decrying William Wilberforce - who pioneered in the British Parliament first, the Act to end the slave trade and then the abolition of slavery itself. Undoubtedly, they would also have used every influence in England to thwart the efforts of Wilberforce and the abolitionists.

Meanwhile, conditions on Antigua for the slave remained appalling resulting in seven revolts and six major conspiracies between 1640 and 1713. Running away was a frequent means of escape from the brutal conditions on Antiguan plantations. Runaways formed a community on Antigua's highest hill, Boggy Peak, and in 1684, the Government posted bounties of £2.10s for the capture of live slaves and £1 for dead ones. In 1688, the militia stormed the camp and burned the leaders to ashes.

*William Wilberforce led the movement to abolish slavery*

*This 18th Century painting depicts West India Docks in London where ships laden with sugar would arrive from the Caribbean*

After the slave trade was abolished in 1807, rebellions became more frequent. This explodes the myth, perpetrated by the apologists for slavery, that slaves were somehow content with their condition. In reality, early slaves - from various tribes and speaking different languages - could not communicate among themselves. Thus, they were unable to discuss their plight, let alone plot an insurrection. This policy of importing slaves from diverse tribes continued for years, the first coming from modern Liberia, Ghana, Togo, Dahomey and western Nigeria. It is the process of 'creolisation' that produced the conditions for slave resistance. After 1807, the majority of slaves, having been born in the Caribbean, were able to communicate with each other and were not constrained by the tribal prejudices of their forebears.

In 1831, just three years before slavery was abolished, there was an insurrectionary movement on Antigua in protest at the prohibition of the 'Negro Sunday Market' at which slaves sold their private production. The insurrection was so widespread that the Governor of Barbados had to send reinforcements to help the militia in Antigua put down the rebellion.

By comparison, the slaves on Barbuda had a relatively easy life if it is possible to discount the reprehensible system of slavery itself. As West Indian historian Douglas Hall notes:

"For the slaves, Barbuda was a relatively happy place. They were engaged, largely in pastoral and hunting occupations or as skilled workers in wood and leather. Many became expert sailors and fishermen. Above all, they were not subject to the tyranny of the cane fields."

Unlike the slaves on Antigua, those on Barbuda "enjoyed an abundance of provisions from their large garden plots, from hunting game in the forests, and from fishing". They had at most three white overseers and lived virtually on their own. Significantly, the Barbudan slaves deeply resented being transferred to Antigua. The first such recorded transfer was in 1779. Even though they

*Slave workforce cutting sugar cane on an Antiguan estate*

were slaves, the Barbudans "adamantly rejected emigration to the Antigua plantations". In 1831, Codrington's manager in Antigua wrote to him explaining that many of the Barbudans died shortly after transfer to the Antigua estates, and he added:

"On Barbuda, they ramble through the woods all hours of the night, taking any thing that comes in their way, either deer, sheep or cattle, as required... They are used to live on fresh meat which they do not get here... When here they cannot stop in their houses at night, but are foraging at all hours, and the air is very different to Barbuda, being damp and chilly, they often take violent colds and fall into dropsy."

23,350 slaves on Antigua were emancipated on 1 August 1834 along with those in The Bahamas and Bermuda. In all of the other British colonies in the Caribbean, there was a four year transition period, called apprenticeship, before full freedom was granted.

But, the immediate emancipation of the slaves was no act of benevolence as will become apparent later in this text.

The freed slaves in Antigua woke up on Emancipation Day as landless wage earners paid the princely sum of one shilling per day. They had nothing except a notional freedom, for they owned nothing and had no choice but to continue working on the sugar plantations of their former masters. And, therein lies the real reason for the full emancipation of the Antiguan slaves without apprenticeship.

The sugar planters received £415,713 from the British Treasury as compensation for the slaves they lost. In addition they obtained a large and captive workforce. Since the slaves had no means of earning a living other than by working on the sugar estates, the plantation owners freed them, paid them a derisory wage and evaded the burden of feeding, clothing and housing them. One planter, at a meeting of proprietors prior to the decision on whether or not to institute a period of apprenticeship, actually proposed full emancipation because it was more profitable. The planter, "produced statements to shew, that under a free system he would have to pay wages to one third only of the negroes whom he should be required to support as apprentices; and that he could work his estates equally well by free labour, at a less expense."

Despite their gain, the planters still took a number of steps to restrict the former slaves on Antigua. First, they passed the Contract Act under which the former slaves were made to sign contracts of employment imposing penalties for breaches. These penalties ranged from loss of wages for minor infractions to imprisonment for what they determined to be major infringements such as missing two days work in a fortnight. Then, they reduced the amount of land on their estates available for workers to cultivate food crops. This made the workers increasingly dependent on their wages to purchase food and therefore tied them more firmly to the sugar estates.

The freedom of the liberated slaves was further constrained in October 1836 with the passage of the Police Act by which the planters prohibited country people from bringing their goods to market without a pass from the manager of the estate on which they resided. Without such a pass, the police were empowered to seize their property. Two Englishmen, who were in Antigua at the time the Act was passed, recorded the following account given to them by a former slave of the importance of selling their produce:

"The wage of one shilling per day was not enough to maintain them. He had a wife and six children, and an old mother to support; of whom, two of the children only were able to earn any thing. They could not manage without "minding" their little stock. He said that if a labourer was five minutes after time in the morning, the manager stopped his pay for the day. He complained also that he had just received thirty days notice to quit because he refused to allow one of his children whom he wished to put to trade, to go to the field, although he promised that all his other children should be brought up to estate labour."

Many of the freed slaves emigrated to Guyana and Trinidad where better wages were being paid for labour on larger and less populated estates. Recognising the haemorrhaging of their exploited labour, the planters on Antigua passed an Act for "preventing clandestine deportation of labourers, artificers, handicraftsmen and domestic servants from the island".

But as the oppressive conditions on the sugar estates continued, so too did migration. This created a shortage of labour in the early 1890s. To meet their need for labour, the planters imported 500 Chinese but, according to one writer, "owing to the absence of contracts, the immigration was not so successful as it might have been, but it relieved the pressure at the time."

It is a tribute to the tenacity and industry of the former slaves that in the four years following emancipation, despite the brutality from which they had recently emerged and the deprivation into which they were delivered, they moved from being landless wage earners to possessors of 1,037 houses in 27 villages. They bought plots of land on hire purchase and met their payments faithfully. After working a full day on the sugar plantations, they went home to cultivate their front and back gardens with plantains, yams, bananas and pineapples. They even found time to grow flowers. Their carefully laid out plots with their pretty gardens can still be seen today in villages such as Liberta, the first of the free villages to be created.

In the meantime, Barbuda was so little remembered in Britain that the draftsmen of the Bill for the Abolition of Slavery had omitted it in the document. Codrington continued to maintain the former slaves on Barbuda, then numbering about 500, but

*Loading barrels of sugar into rowing boats for transfer to ships anchored in Willoughby Bay*

*The boiling house on Delaps Estate*

on 2 April 1860, he wrote a letter addressed to all of them suggesting that they go to work on his estates in Antigua because there was nothing for them to do on Barbuda. They refused.

Paradoxically, the conditions of relative ease which existed for the Barbudans during slavery changed after the Abolition Act was passed.

Sir Bethel Codrington completely freed his slaves on Barbuda in 1834, even though Barbuda had not been listed in the Abolition Law. Having done so, he was faced with the problem that 500 people, now living on his property, were dependent on him but did not belong to him.

Codrington's agent therefore drew up an Agreement in 1835 to deal with this new situation. In summary, the Agreement stated that:

- all workers' provision-grounds were to be sited within a short radius around the village;
- the Barbudans would have the right 'to set Pots and Trammels to catch fish in the Lagoon' - but in no other manner and in no other place without express permission;
- the Barbudans would be allowed to gather cashews and cashew-nuts only from trees growing on their provision-grounds, and even there the proprietor might earmark certain trees for his own use;
- Barbudans could catch crabs at Sand Bank or King's Hall - but nowhere else without express permission;
- labourers were forbidden to trespass or commit injury upon any land, cultivated or not, 'from which they have been hitherto prohibited', under such penalty as the Governor might deem expedient;
- freedom of movement beyond Barbuda was also limited. Any three labourers, at any one time, would be allowed to go to Antigua in one of the Codringtons' vessels in order to sell and buy goods, but they should not stay longer than three days and this privilege could be enjoyed only once in every four months.

This arrangement - while it placed restrictions on the Barbudans that they had not experienced under slavery - did not turn out to be advantageous for the Codringtons. The cost of maintaining the Barbudans proved to be greater than the earnings the island produced. By deed poll executed on 13 July 1870, the Codringtons surrendered their lease 35 years before it was due to expire in 1905. Thus ended the long association between the Codringtons and Barbuda.

In the meantime, the Antigua legislature had been given responsibility for Barbuda in 1858, an obligation they accepted only on the proviso that it would cost them no money. On 1 August, 1860, by an Order-in-Council signed by the British Monarch at the Isle of Wight, Barbuda was annexed to Antigua. Neither the Antigua legislature nor the freed slaves on Barbuda were happy with this development - the former because they felt it would be a burden on their treasury and the latter because they disliked Antigua which, over the years had become a place of punishment in their minds since it was there that the unruly among them were sentenced, and many had died.

The Antiguan authorities tried to free themselves of spending money on Barbuda by leasing the island to new tenants. However, each lease ended in disaster and, finally, in November 1898, Barbuda was once again re-possessed by the Governor of the Leeward Islands and the Antiguan Legislature at last agreed to make financial provision for the island.

However, despite the new travail which the Barbudans experienced with lease-owners of the island, their antagonism toward Antigua did not decline. Indeed, Barbudan hostility to Antigua continued for another hundred years, and was evident when the Government of Antigua and Barbuda sought the country's independence from Britain.

*19th Century impression of the Gracehill Estate*

*The old Court House in St John's*

# CHAPTER SEVEN

# *Bitter sugar*

The fortunes of Britain in the 17th and 18th century may have been made on the sweetness of sugar, but colonial sugar policy in Antigua left the island a bitter legacy.

For over 200 years until the early 1950s, Antigua was deliberately made a monoculture economy - sugar. No attempt was made to introduce any other economic activity and, therefore, the country's fortune was inextricably tied to sugar for good or ill. Such skills as were developed among the people related entirely to the sugar estates. After the 1900s by which time the country's population had grown and prices for cane sugar had dropped, the shortsightedness of this "one crop economy" became evident. But, it had to confront the colonial power, unyielding and ugly, before any quarter was given to the introduction of other agricultural activity. After 1900, corn and cotton cultivation was allowed but sugar still reigned supreme.

Prior to 1834, the sugar plantations were organised on the basis of slave labour so, obviously, there was no question of benefits accruing to the workers. There was little change after slavery was abolished. The workers had no alternative but to return to the plantations to be paid atrociously low wages since all the land was owned by the sugar barons. The estate owners also refused to rent or lease land to the workers for fear that the labour force would be depleted. This unannounced policy continued until the early 1900s. Therefore, labour and land were completely tied up by the sugar barons and no cultivation of food crops was possible.

The estate owners insisted on the importation of food supplies. By this means, they made the workers captive to wages from the sugar estates in order to pay for imported food. Since sugar continued to occupy most of the arable land until 1972. Antigua's food import bill rose astronomically and by 1980 it represented over 25 per cent of the country's total imports in terms of cost.

Significantly, in the latter years of sugar cultivation in Antigua though it was the country's main export, it could not pay for the island's imports so that the balance of trade deficit rose from 0.9 per cent in 1950 to 45.4 per cent in 1970.

Aside from a legacy of very little food production in Antigua, the colonial sugar policy fostered a deliberate decision to ignore the educational development of the people. Between 1834 and 1845, the British Government provided what it called "The Negro Education Grant". The grant was intended to provide basic primary education for the freed slaves and in 1845 it was discontinued as a lever to force the local legislature to provide education facilities on the island. The legislature, dominated by the sugar barons, saw no

*Early 19th Century painting of a distillery on the Weatherell's Estate*

benefit in educating workers needed for their fields and therefore, they simply ignored education altogether. For the next 69 years until 1914, it was the churches which provided basic education for the masses of the people. Finally, in 1914, the legislature agreed to assume responsibility for primary education only and though there were secondary schools for a privileged few - the children of the well-to-do - not a single secondary school was introduced for the masses until the 1950's when, as a result of trade union agitation black people formed the majority in the legislature. Consequently, Antigua has not been able to develop a big enough reservoir of professional skills and now experiences a shortage of skilled and qualified personnel to perform the functions necessary to a growing economy.

Sugar prices began to decline in the 1950s and by the mid-1960s, the industry was in serious financial trouble. The Government was forced to inject $1m simply to keep it afloat and to protect the jobs of some 3,000 workers. But still the Sugar Syndicate would not dispose of the land to Antiguan buyers. It was not until 1967, when sugar was fetching poor prices, that the Syndicate decided to sell. However, even their decision to sell underscored their contempt for the mass of people in Antigua. One estate, Fitches Creek, was earmarked for sale to retired South Africans to be used as residences. The Government had to quickly intervene to stop this plan by pointing out that it was opposed to the system of apartheid in South Africa and had ceased all trading with that country. The Government borrowed over £6m from a Commercial Bank and purchased all the estates.

To protect the jobs of the workers, safeguard the livelihood of peasant cane farmers and avoid importation of sugar, the Government maintained the sugar estates

*An early painting showing slave huts in the Gambles district on the outskirts of St John's. The building in the background is the original St John's Cathedral as it looked before it was destryoed by a hurricane in 1843*

until 1971 when they were closed down, leaving 60 per cent of Antigua's arable land uncultivated.

Since then, the Government has attempted to diversify the agricultural base of the economy by utilising the land for the production of corn/sorghum, cotton and food crops.

In the early 1980s an attempt was made to reintroduce sugar production for domestic consumption, but the memories of worker exploitation in sugar's interest was ingrained in the minds of Antiguans; they would not return to the industry and foreign labour had to be imported. In addition, the costs of rehabilitating the factory and fields were too expensive. The experiment quickly died.

Sugar's legacy proved to be too bitter for Antigua.

*The 'Negro Sunday Market' where home-grown produce would be sold*

*Antigua Sailing Week*

# CHAPTER EIGHT

# Paradise encountered

Antigua is famous for its international sailing regatta - Sailing Week - once a year when yachts from all over the world flock to Antigua for a week of challenging competition on the sea.

No day during this week is complete without some form of participation in the five gruelling races held every year during the last week of April. Starting off as entertainment for local yachtsmen, in 1964 British Overseas Airways Corporation (British Airways) donated a silver cup for the winner of the race between Guadeloupe and Antigua. Encouraged by this acknowledgement, the organisers decided in 1967 to hold three more days of racing in three classes: racing, cruising and traditional. Since then, Sailing Week has not looked back. From 1968, the number of entries multiplied with yachts from all over the world. Soon entries had to be limited to 150.

The races are a test of skill and endurance, followed avidly by hundreds of visitors, who now flock to Antigua for the event, and thousands of locals, who seize vantage points along the coast, to witness world champion yachts rubbing hulls with others less known but just as ambitious. While Sailing Week provides good fun on the sea, it is just as good an opportunity for revelry on shore. End-of-race beach parties attract sailors and spectators alike in a haze of booze, music and good fellowship. But,

much of the shore activities is reserved for the last day when the daring try to walk the greasy pole with many ending up in the sea; men and women join in the nautical tug-o-war, quenching their thirst in the beer drinking competition; and the rubber raft race always produces a few sailors rendered legless by more than a few generous tots of rum.

The centre of this activity is Nelson's Dockyard at English Harbour. The dockyard is named after Admiral Lord Horatio Nelson, the British Hero of the Battle of Trafalgar during the Napoleonic wars between England and France. Nelson arrived in Antigua in 1784 at the age of 26 and stayed for three years. The house in which he lived is now a museum. He was Senior Naval Captain at the time in command of a Frigate, Boreas. He returned there in 1805 to provision his ship on his way to defeat Villeneuve at Trafalgar and so carve a permanent place for his name in the history books of the world.

But English Harbour's importance preceded Nelson - in 1725 it was selected along with Port Royal in Jamaica as one of the permanent naval stations in the Caribbean. The development of the area was the idea of Captain Arthur Delgarno of H.M.S. South Sea Castle who argued that "English Harbour might be made a very proper place for careening and refitting, and so save HM ships the trouble of travelling to the Northern Colonies for that purpose." So grateful to Delgarno was the expatriate British community in Antigua, the Antigua Assembly voted him 200 guineas with, "our most sincere thanks for the great benefit you have done us, in making the wharf and platform at English Harbour, a place by nature fitted, and by a law of our country appropriated, for the reception of His Majesty's ships of war, and by you, sir, rendered more safe and commodious for that purpose".

Nelson did not have a pleasant stay at English Harbour. A young and zealous officer, he decided to vigorously enforce the British Navigation Act which stipulated that there should be no trading between the former American colonies and the British Empire. Despite the stipulation a roaring trade was taking place between the American states and Antigua and Nevis. Nelson, not yet matured to the political realities of life, arrested ships and seized their cargo off Nevis. He also uncovered customs frauds perpetrated by merchants in St John's and the Agent Victualler in St John's. He lost no time in reporting these frauds to London. In the course of these events, he quarrelled with the Governor, General Shirley, and he was ostracised by merchants and plantation owners on Antigua.

The Antigua and Nevis merchants had considerable influence in London and they mounted an effective lobby against Nelson who was forced to drop his fraud charges. Further, year after year passed with no new appointment to a ship. Nelson began to talk of "becoming a naval mercenary in the service of the Tsar of Russia." Discussion of his "high-handed officiousness" while stationed at English Harbour had earned him a reputation of a trouble-maker. Five years went by before Nelson was finally recalled to naval service. Had the reputation he earned at English Harbour triumphed over England's need for seasoned Captains in the Napoleonic war, Nelson would have been denied his victory at the battle of Trafalgar and history might have been written rather differently.

Situated in an old volcano cone, English Harbour is made up of virtually land-locked basins with only a narrow passage to the sea - this protected it both from the weather and from sightings from the sea. It was to defend this naturally strategic location that fortifications were built, between 1780 and 1790, on the overhanging mountain ridges by order of General Thomas Shirley when he became Captain General and Governor-in-Chief of the Leeward Islands. The ruins of those fortifications at what is now called Shirley Heights can still be seen today. There too is Clarence House - a graceful Georgian house overlooking the Dockyard. It was built in 1787 for the use of the Captain of HMS Pegasus, Prince William Henry, the Duke of Clarence, who later became King William IV of England in 1830. Later, the house was occupied by the Commissioner of the Dockyard and Governors of the island subsequently used it as a country house. Princess Margaret, the sister of Queen Elizabeth II, stayed there for a short visit on her honeymoon in 1960.

Nonetheless, the volcano cone presented great problems for human health. As a surgeon in 1808 reported, "more seamen die here every year than in the whole Leeward Island station besides, with the exception of Barbados. The causes of fever here are accumulated: the men are employed at severe labour in the dockyard beneath a vertical sun: and in spite of the severest discipline find the means of procuring rum, a temptation no sailor can withstand."

The tombstones in the cemetery on Shirley Heights overlooking the Dockyard still tell the tale of illnesses which led many a young sailor to find a permanent resting place on Antigua.

The naval barracks and the Dockyard at English Harbour were abandoned by the British Admiralty in 1889. For a few years it was used as a port-of-call by the inter-colonial

*Spectators watch the 'Between the Legs' competition at the Antigua Yacht Club on Lay Day during Antigua Sailing Week, 1998*

*Beer Drinking race during Lay Day at the Yacht Club*

mail steamers, then in 1906 it was handed over to the local Government which, for lack of funds, allowed it to fall into disrepair.

In May 1951, the Governor of Antigua at the time launched the Society of Friends of English Harbour to restore Nelson's Dockyard. Among the influential "friends" were Lady Churchill, the wife of Britain's former Prime Minister Winston Churchill who visited in 1961, and Prince Phillip and Princess Margaret, the husband and sister of Queen Elizabeth II.

Many of the buildings have now been restored, and the area accommodates hotels, restaurants and shops. The Dockyard, with the house in which Nelson occasionally slept during the three years he was stationed in Antigua, is spectacular, and the ruins at Shirley Heights permits the visitor to meander through naval facilities and fortifications which open an interesting vista on British naval history. At nearby Dow's Hill, the National Parks Authority maintains the Interpretation Centre where an audiovisual show provides a brief history of Antigua. The views of the area from Dow's Hill are breathtakingly beautiful.

Looking out from Shirley Heights at the panorama of English Harbour, Falmouth Harbour and the broad sweep inland, it is obvious how the country was shorn of its trees - the mountain sides are bare and harsh with only the hardy acacia plants holding the soil together. Throughout the countryside, apart from occasional coconut and breadfruit trees, it is the sturdy acacia with its gnarled branches and yellow blossoms that brings relief to dry and dusty plains.

But, along the coast the perfection of nature in the majestic bays and coves make up for the imperfections of man which led the sugar cane planters to destroy the forest cover of the land. The waters in Willoughby Bay and Half Moon Bay, Mosquito Cove and Hawksbill, run turquoise, green and blue - wondrous spectacles causing even the hardened to catch a breath.

No day is complete without seeing the Capital, St John's. It is congested in a friendly way. For even though most of the shops are tiny and the sidewalks are narrow, there is no feeling of pressure. Life moves on in a laid-back, relaxed atmosphere. The shops are full to overflowing with stock, and the noise of the traffic and conversations is punctuated with the rhythms pouring out of a record store or from a building where a live band may be rehearsing.

The town started around a Fort whose construction began on Rat Island in 1672. In 1683 the first St John's Church was built and soon the community which moved to the area grew in size. A market was built in 1702 and cross streets were laid out with broad avenues running east and west. These avenues were joined by narrower north and south cross streets. "This scheme", one expert has observed, "provided for the main facades to typically face north or south to the broad avenues."

The institutional buildings were put in place in the early 19th century: Government House in 1801 and a General Post Office in 1850. The mid 19th century was a period of great construction activity in St John's following a fire in 1841 which devastated many buildings. The result of different eras of construction has left the town a blend of architectural styles: Georgian, Victorian, Romantic and International.

The pedestrian in St John's faces many challenges, not least of which is the appearance and disappearance of very narrow sidewalks. This situation arises from the manner in which the town's buildings were constructed. Some buildings virtually hug the street. One resident in 1842 recorded that St John's, "had no causeways (sidewalks) and consequently the pedestrian has to elbow his way amid trucks, handbarrows, gigs, carriages and horsemen, droves of cattle or cargoes of mules just landed from other countries, cattle carts or moving houses".

Newer buildings were forced to have sidewalks, but inevitably they are narrow and

*Sunset at Dickenson Bay during Antigua Sailing Week, 1998*

not continuous. Therefore, today the pedestrian frequently steps from sidewalk to roadside amid parked cars, moving cargo, and a constant flow of other people. But, far from being threatening, the atmosphere is exhilarating, filled with a great sense of life and healthy activity; a sense that is redoubled by the brightness of the sun's light and the warmth of its glow.

"Moving houses" are also encountered upon occasion, except that today these tiny cottages are transported by tractor and trailer, whereas in 1842 they were set on carts and pulled by oxen.

Two St John's development projects known as Heritage Quay and Redcliffe Quay, have replaced slum areas with buildings which recall the architectural form of the mid 19th century. The panoply of structures, outlined by attractive promenades, are as eye catching collectively as they are significant in their individual representation of ages past and present.

Redcliffe Quay and Heritage Quay are both worth visiting. Both Quays are filled with shops and restaurants, and while duty-free shopping is available in Heritage Quay, the shops in Redcliffe Quay are a virtual Aladdin's Cave of fabrics, knick-knacks, quality garments and unusual curios from the Caribbean and Latin America. Redcliffe Quay in particular creates the illusion of transporting the wanderer into the past. The layout of the area and the structures and architectural designs of its buildings generate a calming effect upon the spirit.

Heritage Quay may lack the West Indian ambience of Redcliffe Quay, but its air conditioned shops readily compensate. On a hot day, it is a welcome relief to stroll through the shops of this Quay which starts on the sea at a new deep water harbour - where cruise shops release their thousands of passengers directly into the shopping centre - and ends at the beginning of St John's. The quay encompasses shops of every kind - expensive jewellery, designer clothes and luggage, liquor and wines, craft and crystal. The prices are competitive with the best duty-free ports in the Caribbean, and bargains are readily available.

Antigua was an important sugar producing island in the 18th and 19th centuries, St John's has always been a busy commercial capital. Fort James once defended the entrance to St John's Harbour. The original fortification was built about 1675, but most of the buildings seen today were started in 1749, and the laying of the foundation was celebrated with full monastic rites. By the time of the American Revolution, there were 36 guns here, and accommodation for 70 men. In the 19th century, a gun was fired at sunrise and at sunset, and salutes were fired for visiting warships. There are ten cannons at the Fort today. They weigh about two tonnes each and can fire one and a half miles. Twelve men were required to handle each gun.

The Old Court House now accommodates a historical Museum and is well worth visiting. The building was built of freestone from Long Island, Guiana Island and Pelican Island in 1747. It was severely damaged by the great earthquake of 1843 and later restored. Besides normal court house functions, balls, dinners, bible meetings and charity sales were also held there. It was again damaged by earthquake in 1974, and reconstructed in the early 1980s.

St John's Police Station was built in 1754 on Market Street as a guard house and jail. Four years later an arsenal was added to provide a central place for the storage of munitions. It is said that the prisoners used to hold conversations with the passers-by in Newgate Street, and spread evil advice to the members of both sexes who loiter in the area. Then in 1831 the jail was moved to the barracks east of town, where it still is today. Old bayonets capping the railings of the courtyard, were placed there when the militia was disbanded in 1838. The arsenal was used up to the 1930s and Antigua's old records were kept in vaulted stone rooms that were once the cells of the jail.

'Posing off' in the Parade of Bands during Carnival

Nearby is St John's Cathedral. As it is today, the Cathedral was built after the great earthquake of 1843 and consecrated in 1848. The first St John's Church was built in 1681, and this was replaced about 1722. It played an active part in the island's life, and was used in 1805 for the investiture of Admiral Hood by Lord Lavington. Just as pleas were being made for the church to be elevated to the status of Cathedral, the earthquake struck. The present Cathedral's interior is encased in wood in order to protect it from both hurricane and earthquake damage. This was put to good use when another earthquake struck in 1974. It is an unusual and interesting building architecturally, with two towers in a baroque style.

Not far from the Cathedral is one of the newer buildings on Antigua. Donated to the country by international businessman and philanthropist, Bruce Rappaport, and his wife Ruth, the building houses the Antigua and Barbuda Archives and serves as a repository for historical documents and as a display centre of the country's history.

The Prison is across the road from the Archives building. It was built in 1735 after a fund was raised to build barracks for the 38th Regiment of Foot, which was stationed in Antigua from 1707 to 1764. The present grammar school was then a hospital, and beautiful gardens with ponds, orange groves, Turk's Head cacti and a skittle alley were situated between these two building. It was not until 1831 that the barracks was converted to its present use as a prison.

Opposite the Prison is the Antigua Recreation Ground - venue for Caribbean and international cricket and football matches. Antiguans have been able to watch two of their native sons - Vivian Richards and Richie Richardson - captain the West Indies Cricket Team to victory there. They have also seen other Antiguans like Andy Roberts, Curtley Ambrose, Kenneth Benjamin and Winston Benjamin, break into the West Indies Team through natural and graceful talent.

Sport in Antigua is pursued with an ardency that borders on religious zeal. Everywhere on the island, cricket matches will be encountered in open fields, on the beaches and on well established cricket grounds. For some, the achievement of world class status is a serious motivation. They have seen Richards, Richardson, Roberts, Ambrose and the Benjamins achieve a good living from the game. But, for most, the impetus is the pure love of cricket which Tim Hector asserts shaped "the vital character, the essential nature of the people of Antigua."

Football ranks second in the sports fanaticism of Antiguans, and, like cricket, games are played in every nook and cranny of the island, although Antigua is yet to produce a world class player. Increasingly, basketball has become a popular sport with floodlit courts across the island attracting players well into the night. Great interest is also taken in Boxing although, for lack of facilities, it is not pursued in Antigua. Yet, Maurice Hope moved from Antigua to England, where training facilities are available, and rose to be the light middleweight Boxing champion of the world.

The Antigua Recreation Ground is home to Antigua's participation in international cricket and football matches, but it was also there that the country's first national hero, Prince Klaas, a Coromantee slave of royal birth from the Gold Coast (Ghana), who conspired to start a rebellion, was tortured and killed in 1736. He was strapped to a wheel and his bones broken one by one. It is said that he died with great fortitude. Four others were broken on the wheel, six were 'put out to dry' (hung in chains without food), and 58 were burnt at the stake, many in Otto's Pasture on the edge of St John's.

While bodies died that day the spirit which sought freedom lives on and is given expression in Carnival in Antigua and Caribana in Barbuda when the rich culture

of the two islands are celebrated in a festival of music, song and dance. It is also at the Antigua Recreation Ground that Carnival shows and calypso contests are held. Carnival is always during the last week of July and the first week in August coinciding with the abolition of slavery on 1 August, 1834.

Antigua and Barbuda has a rich cultural blend of English tradition, American influence and African atavism. These have all been woven into a unique West Indian tapestry that goes beyond music, dance and art. The culture of Antiguans and Barbudans encompasses the many facets of daily life. It is recognisable in the way bowlers run up to the wicket in a game of cricket, there is almost an abandon of movement, a relaxed, jaunty hurling of the legs, a rhythm in the body language that is pure poetry; a woman simply walking down the street reflects that culture in the generous swing of her hips and the freedom of her laughter, two men talking to each other display their culture in animated gesturing with their hands and the expressive demeanour of their faces; words are never adequate in the West Indian conversation.

When the Africans were brought to Antigua and Barbuda, they may have been stripped of their own cultural grounding, but they did not simply adopt the culture of the coloniser wholesale. Instead, they adapted and refined it until it became peculiarly theirs. The most compelling example of this is the reverential playing of classical music on steel drums with the flair and fullness of a symphony orchestra.

Part of the culture of the country is the people's interest and awareness of events in the outside world. The ordinary man in the street will discuss the Middle East as confidently and knowledgeably as he would events in his own village. And on cricket, every Antiguan and Barbudan will hold forth with an authority born of tracing any match worth recalling.

Nowhere is the abundance of talent more prevalent, however, than in the calypso. It is the calypso competition that brings out the true spirit of the Antiguan and Barbudan personality, for the calypso performance is theatre masking serious commentary on local and international events and entertaining recitations of human relationships and behaviour. The lyrics are cleverly written, combining rhyme and rhythm with wit. No one and nothing is safe from the scathing attention of the calypsonians who, throughout Carnival and Caribana, occupy pride of place in the hearts of the people.

The high point of Carnival is the selection of the Calypso King of the year. Antigua and Barbuda has produced some extremely gifted calypsonians in King Short-Shirt, King Obstinate, The Mighty Swallow, Chalice and others. The renditions of the calypsonians are quickly embraced by the steel drums and competition is intense on the selection of the calypso to be used as the "road march". This march, most inappropriately named, is a mass street "jump up" by thousands of people in extravagant costumes accompanied by vibrant steelband music and gaily decorated floats.

Culture in Antigua and Barbuda is also an amazingly unifying force, and Carnival plays a special role in that regard. At the carnival shows and in the street "jump ups", politicians and others locked in rivalry all year round drop their differences and in the spirit of camaraderie which characterises this annual festival, jump up together in the streets and actually joke with each other at bars and booths on the carnival grounds. Such are the wonders performed by this unique cultural experience.

But what a season Carnival and Caribana bring! Music rings out everywhere throughout the periods leading up to scheduled events. By Carnival J'Ouvert morning, people from all walks of life are ready for a day of non-stop dancing through the streets, intoxicated with the driving music and the atmosphere of total abandon.

*Supa Stars steel band, Carnival 1998*

There is a deliberate effort to involve children with the Children's Carnival and the Mr and Miss Teenage Pageant Contests - not that they needed encouragement, for officially involved or not, children are ready participants in the joy of life which the festivals bring.

Outside of St John's there are a number of interesting buildings that tell something of the history of Antigua. It is worth the trouble to see St George's Church in Fitches Creek. The original Chapel of Ease is believed to have been built about 1687, on land granted to Daniel Fitch. This was later transferred to the Byam family, whose family is buried there. The Church was remodelled in 1735, and has been changed very little since then. Some of the tablets date back as far as 1695. In this year a William Barnes was buried there, the first settler to be buried in a place of worship. Some of the silver in the church is very old. A planter, Lucy Blackman, left money for the purchase of silver plate in 1724.

Parham Church in the village of Parham has been described as "the finest church in the British West Indies". It was built in the 1840's after the original wooden church near Parham Hill had been burnt down. It was designed by Thomas Weeks, a famous architect, and is a beautiful and unusual design. It is a very important building, and has recently undergone considerable restoration.

Fig Tree Drive offers no buildings of special significance, but it is the most thickly wooded area of Antigua. Starting at Sweets Village, it goes through a deep defile between tall hills in the middle of the island towards Curtain Bluff Hotel. The height of the area combined with the overhanging trees provides a cool atmosphere set in lush, verdant surroundings. The drive takes its name from the small local bananas - figs - which grow in abundance in the area. Other fruit trees in profusion are the breadfruit, mango and tamarind. Fig Tree Drive provides a captivating insight into the terrain of Antigua before it was shorn of its trees and vegetation in the service of sugar cane production.

A United States Naval Base and Air Force Tracking Station on Antigua is unavoidable. They command an area between Hodges Bay and Coolidge where the Airport is located. The base is inaccessible without an invitation, but many of its buildings and its very large satellite tracking station are plainly visible. The United States first gained access to this facility in 1940 when Britain granted ninety-nine year leases in exchange for fifty US destroyers. The arrangement was modified by the US-UK Mutual Defence Assistance Treaty in 1950. Since then, the Government of Antigua and Barbuda has entered sovereign arrangements with the United States Government for the continued use of the base at an annual fee. The Government uses the income from the base to service external debts.

The naval base was used by the US as part of its Sound Surveillance System (SONUS) antisubmarine programme. SONUS is reportedly "a worldwide network of fixed hydrophones that rest on the continental shelf, detect submarine movement, and send the information via satellite to the United States." The airforce tracking station is said to be utilised as part of the US space programme and is used for tracking space flights.

When the base was started in 1941, it provided better and higher paid jobs to Antiguans than were then available to them. Many were freed from the sugar plantations by securing jobs there. They also learned some technical skills that would otherwise have not been possible. While the base and the tracking station do not provide as many jobs to locals as they used to, there is obvious local regard for the role it once played. Even though the Government has been criticised from time to time by political forces outside of Antigua for allowing the United States to maintain a base there, the country continues to provide a hospitable environment for it.

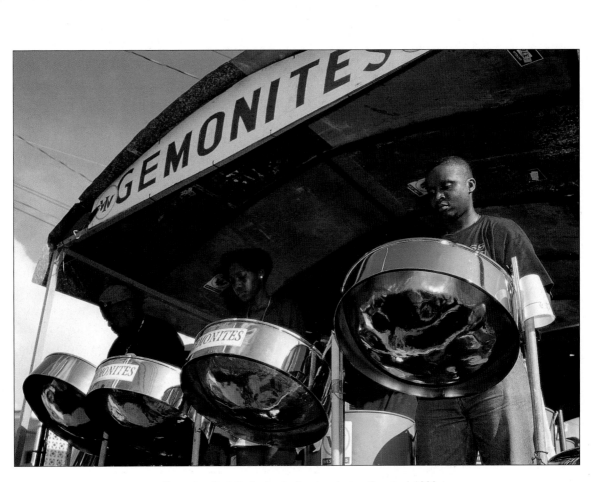

*Gemonites Steel Orchestra performing during Carnival 1998*

*Miss Antigua and Jaycees Caribbean Queen 1998, flanked by local queen contestants*

Barbuda presents a special charm. Today, the island represents the nearest any one will get to seeing a West Indian island that is unspoilt. Deer and wild pig still roam freely in the scrub and theirs is the only footprint likely to be found on some beaches. Flying there is a 20 minute journey from Antigua's V C Bird International Airport. Landing is either at the airstrip at Codrington, the capital of Barbuda, or at the private airstrip at Coco Point Lodge. Apart from the magnificent beaches and crystal clear waters for swimming, lazing, snorkelling and scuba diving, the Martello Tower and Fort are very interesting. Built at the main landing place for Codrington, the tower and fort defended the southwestern approach to Barbuda and ships anchored off the landing. The tower was also used as a lookout and signal station, especially for the reporting of shipwrecks, which were a major income to the Codringtons when they leased the island. Nine guns were once placed in the embrasures. Today there is a fine view from the top, the tower being 56 feet high.

Highland House is situated on the highest point (128 feet) of Barbuda. It is believed to have been built in the 1720's and was occupied on and off by the Codrington family until 1790's. All that remains today are the ruins of a large complex that contained the main house, slave quarters, stables, offices and cisterns. However, the breathtaking view of the northern half of Barbuda is superb.

Several thousand frigate birds have found a sanctuary on Barbuda. The birds are quite majestic - their black colour is relieved by a red pouch which they inflate during nesting as a defence. Their nests are just a few feet above water, and since the birds have no fear of people they can be observed at a close distance. The approach to the sanctuary is by boat from Codrington village airport, and a visit there completes a tour of this naturally beautiful island where animals and birds still live in the wild.

There is not much on Redonda and it is difficult to understand why any but the extremely curious would want to go there. However, there is a man who says he is King of this volcanic rock where his only subjects are birds which, tired from flight, land upon it mostly to perform their ablutions before taking off for more beneficial places. Cedric Boston is a native of Montserrat who read law and politics at the University of Keele in England and was called to the Bar (made a Barrister) at Grays Inn. As King Cedric I, Boston says he gained the crown with the agreement of the nobles of the Court of King Juan I. This rather implausible story has actually been published in a book entitled, 'The Kingdom of Redonda, 1865-1990'.

King Juan 11 - actually the writer Jon M Wynne Tyson of Sussex, England - says that in 1865 Matthew Dowdy Shiel sailed by Redonda and bristling with the pride of recent fatherhood, claimed it as a kingdom for his son. The boy was duly brought to the island and officially proclaimed King Phillipe 1. Upon his death, the throne was bequeathed to the poet, John Gawsworth who appointed several eminent writers such as Dylan Thomas, Ellery Queen, J B Priestly and Lawrence Durrell to various royal positions.

Gasworth became King Juan 1 passing the Kingdom to Wynne Tyson who declared himself King Juan 11. However, in February 1984 Cedric Boston claimed the Kingdom and was declared Cedric I by followers of Gawsworth on the basis that (i) they could not find Wynne-Tyson, and (ii) since Matthew Dowdy Shiel and his son were born in Montserrat like Cedric Boston, and Montserrat's population is only 1,200 Boston and Shiel must be related, giving Boston a hereditary claim to the throne.

Despite all this, no government of Antigua and Barbuda has taken the 'Kingdom' seriously since, so far, not even the birds of Redonda have been asked to bend a knee to the royal authority of King Cedric 1 or his predecessors.

*The Legacy Mas Troupe on Carnival Tuesday*

*Leader of the Band of the
Vitus Mas Troupe
parading through St John's
on Carnival Monday*

*J'Ouvert Morning on Redcliffe Street*

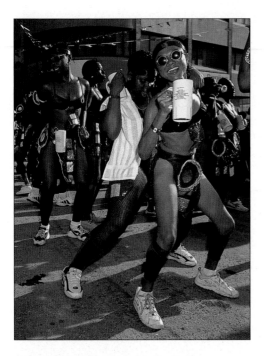

*Legacy's 'Illusion' approaches the Antigua
Recreation Ground for the Judging of the Bands*

*J'Ouvert Morning on Redcliffe Street, St John's*

*'Push it Back' with Dynamics Mas Group*

*Moco Jumbies tower above
the Parade of Bands*

*Carnival is for all ages*

*Little Bees on Carnival Monday*

*Troupes already judged pack the stands of
the Antigua Recreation Ground to cheer on
other bands as they enter Carnival City*

*'Burning Flames' leads the
crowd through Redcliffe
Street on J'Ouvert Morning*

*St John's Cathedral in the capital*

# CHAPTER NINE

# *Dawn of a new day*

In the first century of the post-emancipation period, the people of Antigua and Barbuda suffered from extreme poverty and neglect. Only minimal attention was given to the economic and social well-being of the workers. The legislative assembly was controlled by the planters who also controlled the government. Laws were passed by the planters for the planters, and the majority of the people were their victims. They had no vote, little right of redress for grievances and even less hope of peacefully changing the situation.

The response of the workers to their low wages and bad conditions of employment was work stoppages or strikes. And, when strikes were outlawed by the planters' laws, sabotage took their place - fields were burnt and estate equipment was destroyed. In 1918, a riot ensued during which 15 people were shot, 12 females and three male. Three of them - two men and a woman - subsequently died.

Workers' resentment to the appallingly poor wages paid for long hours of work, inadequate medical attention and unhygienic living conditions continued to fester for decades. But, in the 1930s when the bottom dropped out of the economy because of poor prices for sugar on the world market, Antigua was ready for violent change. Novelle Richards, an eye witness to these events, described the situation as follows:

"The island had staked everything on sugar and it was not only bad prices that had to be faced but the inevitable drought that resulted in disastrous crops. Antigua was a land of misery and depression, an island of slums and hovels, of barefooted, unkempt people."

Appalling conditions for workers were not unique to Antiguans and Barbudans - they existed throughout the West Indies. Everywhere the workers reacted in the same way - strikes, sabotage and riots.

Forced to deal with a cauldron of discontent, the British Government dispatched a Commission under Lord Moyne to investigate conditions in the West Indies. What they saw horrified them. In Antigua, they found that wages were atrocious ranging around four pence a day for women and ten pence for men. Workers toiled long and arduous hours from six in the morning to six at night. At some villages, the Commission was witness to desperate conditions - homes were built of wattle cut from bush, and trash from the field covered the roof. Floors were often just the earth. In some villages and particularly in the poorer areas around St John's, there was great overcrowding with

*St John's in the early 1930s*

as many as eight people living in one small house. Windows were eaten by termites as were doors. Crocus bags were used at night to cover doorways and windows to protect against insects.

Staggered by these terrifying conditions, one of the members of the Commission, Sir Walter Citrine held a public meeting in the Anglican Cathedral school room in St John's on 3 January 1939. Citrine was then President of the Trade Union Council in Britain. He urged the formation of a trade union movement to organise the labour force and secure their rights. On 16 January 1939 an Executive was elected to form the Union. It was not, however, until 3 March 1940 that the union was registered under the name Antigua Trades and Labour Union (AT&LU). Reginald Stevens, a jeweller, was the initial president of the body.

That meeting marked the dawn of a new day in the history of Antigua. It was the point at which the veil of slavery and exploitation, which had hung over the Antiguans for three centuries was finally lifted, and the people began to look forward to genuine citizenship in a free society.

It also launched the career of a man who would dominate every aspect of Antiguan and Barbudan life for the next 50 years. Vere Cornwall Bird was elected as an executive member of the AT&LU at that fateful meeting on 16 January. A former Salvation Army Captain and then small businessman, Bird was elevated to the Presidency of the Union in 1943. He was subsequently to become the first Chief Minister in 1961, the first Premier in 1967, and the first Prime Minister when, on 1 November 1981, Antigua and Barbuda attained full independence from Britain.

Within three months the Union's membership numbered 3,000 and by 1956 its 44 branches in industry and trade totalled 12,712 due-paying members including domestic servants, tradesmen, shop owners, teachers, civil servants and peasant farmers.

In 1946, the Union, under Bird's leadership, recognised that while organised labour had achieved better conditions for workers, change was limited since political authority rested in the Executive Council which was dominated by the plantocrats. A candidate for a parliamentary seat at that time was required to be a property owner. Fortunately for the Union it could produce people with the necessary qualification and in the 1946 General Elections it ran five candidates all of whom were duly elected. Those men were V C Bird, E H Lake, E Williams, Leonard Benjamin and Hugh O. Pratt. Despite the fact that five union representatives were elected, only one, V C Bird, was selected to serve on the Executive Council but "while his views were respected, very few of his suggestions were implemented." The Union, however, was determined to place political power in the hands of the people and agitated for constitutional reform. By 1951 there was full adult suffrage in Antigua without qualification of income or literacy test. The Union selected eight candidates to contest the elections and all won their seats.

In 1956, a ministerial system of government was introduced and in the General Elections of the year, the union again won all eight of the elective seats. However, this election was significant because it saw the rise of a new political party of professional Antiguans who had graduated from universities abroad. The party made no impression on the electorate. In elections in 1961 and 1966, these professionals emerged in parties of different names, but the result was the same; solid rejection by the electorate.

1961 saw further constitutional advances for Antigua with the elected membership of the Legislative Council increasing from eight to ten and the position of Chief Minister being created. The Union won all the elected seats easily and for the first time Barbuda was made a constituency. Prior to

*Vere Cornwall Bird in his early twenties*

1961, Barbuda was attached to St. John's as one constituency. V C Bird was appointed Chief Minister and the pathway to Antigua's independence was cleared.

Conditions in the country had improved during this time, as a result of the trade union's militancy: a fact which was noted by Sir Kenneth Blackburne, Governor of the Leeward Island from 1950 to 1957, in a speech to the Antigua Legislature six years after his arrival:

"All of us who were in Antigua when the last council was opened five years ago can remember the conditions under which the people of this island were then living. We can remember the trickle of muddy water which emerged intermittently and reluctantly from our clogged pipes; when the children in our schools could not sit down because of lack of room; when there was here in St. John's, rows of filthy hovels in which human beings were living in indescribable conditions."

By 1965, the island had made sufficient progress for its leaders to consider independence for Antigua and Barbuda. At this time, there was still only one trade union - the AT&LU - and it was the union representative who formed the Government. In a manifesto for the 1965 General Elections, the union representatives declared their intention to seek independence for Antigua and stated that neither the size of the country nor population constituted an obstacle. The people, once again, gave the union leaders overwhelming support and every seat was won including Barbuda whose representative was McChesney George. In the new Government established by V C Bird, McChesney George was appointed Minister without Portfolio and given responsibility for development in Barbuda.

A Constitutional Conference was held in London in 1966, attended by an Antiguan Government delegation led by V C Bird and including McChesney George. From this conference Antigua with its dependencies Barbuda and Redonda became an Associated State in February 1967. Under this system Antigua was entirely independent in all its internal affairs, but foreign affairs and defence remained under the control of the British. Thus ended over 300 years of colonialism: the people of Antigua and Barbuda were free to conduct their affairs as they saw fit.

Two developments later occurred which threw the country into turmoil. First some of the leaders on Barbuda led by McChesney George, who had been dismissed from the AT&LU by the Executive, began to agitate for the separation of Barbuda from Antigua. The consequences of this will be detailed later in this section.

Second, between 1967 and 1971, Antigua and Barbuda experienced a political upheaval which broke the hold of the AT&LU. In the mid 1950s, opposition to Bird and the Union emerged amongst the professional and business classes who fielded candidates in the elections of 1956, 1961 and 1966 but were roundly defeated at all of them. However, in 1968, the

*The capital as it was in the 1930s with St John's Cathedral in the background*

114

*Britain's former Prime Minister, Winston Churchill, visited Antigua in 1961. He is pictured, left, being greeted by the Governor, Sir Kenneth Blackburne and the Chief Minister, V.C. Bird*

*Following his visit to Antigua, Winston Churchill travelled to Jamaica from where he wrote this letter to V.C. Bird*

*V.C. Bird at the Constitutional talks held in London in 1966 which led to Antigua becoming the first Associated State in the Caribbean. He is flanked by Donald Halstead (left) who later became a member of the opposition, and Arthur Bottomley, Britain's Minister for Commonwealth Affairs*

solidarity amongst the working class, which was the backbone of Bird's strength, ended with the formation of the Antigua Workers Union (AWU) by disgruntled members of the AT&LU, led by its former General Secretary, George Walter. A new political face also appeared on the scene at this time, Leonard Tim Hector. He became an Executive member of the AWU and when the union created a political party, the Progressive Labour Movement (PLM), Hector was made Chairman. He was instrumental in planning and organising a demonstration against the Government in 1968 on recognition for the AWU. Hector resigned a year later saying that the party had campaigned on a policy statement he had devised, but they then abandoned it for expediency. In 1970, George Walter was elected leader of the PLM and in 1971 it won the general elections. Walter became Premier.

The defeat of V C Bird and his band of trade union leaders was surprising. Much had obviously been done to improve conditions in Antigua: workers were receiving better wages, tourism and some manufacturing had been attracted to the country, and a deep water harbour had been built as had an airstrip capable of accepting modern jet aircraft. Two issues appeared to be the cause of V C Bird's defeat: first, the Government had been forced to buy the sugar estates that were facing closure by the Syndicate of private owners. The AT&LU represented the workers and Walter, as General Secretary, faced the brunt of demands for more pay. However, as Head of the Government, Bird knew that increased wages were not possible in an industry that was attracting only poor prices. The conflict between government, as the employer, and the union, as the workers representative, could

*The 1971 General Election was won by the Progressive Labour Movement and the Party's leader, George Walter, became the new Premier of the nation. He is pictured (second from left, seated) with his government and members of the Opposition*

not be reconciled. The workers chose to support Walter. In so doing, they joined forces with the business and professional class who had long opposed the AT&LU - the combination undid the AT&LU's electoral chances.

The PLM, however, served only one term in office. The term coincided with unprecedented high prices for oil which affected tourism and sent the country's import bills sky-rocketing - the effect was devastating. Few governments, especially new and inexperienced ones, survive such economic ill fortune. The sugar industry was closed down on the basis that it had become uneconomic to operate; an oil refinery established in 1965 was shut down; and tourism, which the Bird Government had been nurturing since 1960, also slumped. But apart from the economic collapse, the PLM passed legislation which provided its opponents with a rallying

point. Among the legislation were the Public Order Act which effectively put an end to opposition political activity, and the Newspaper Amendment Act, which closed down every newspaper in the country and stifled freedom of expression and speech.

These policies attracted vocal opposition from a new breed of men in the AT&LU and from Tim Hector who had become the leader of the Antigua Caribbean Liberation Movement (ACLM), a party he had helped to form.

It was during this period of the PLM Government that the ALP began to constitute itself as a genuine political party. At a convention in 1972, Lester Bird - second son of V C Bird - was elected Chairman, with John St Luce as General Secretary. Lester Bird had returned from London as an Attorney; John St Luce was a graduate of the London School of Economics. V C Bird remained political

Leader and Ernest Emmanuel Williams led the Party in Parliament.

The principal organisers of the ALP were Lester Bird, John St Luce and Hugh Marshall. Since his return to Antigua in 1970, Lester Bird had established a good reputation as a lawyer and was elected as President of the Antigua Cricket Association where his organisational skills became apparent as did his gift for amiability. Along with Marshall and St Luce, he carried the political fight to the Government organising opposition and voicing dissent through Radio ZDK which was owned by the Bird family.

By 1974, a right-wing political party - the Antigua Progressive Party - led by Rowan Henry merged with the ALP and produced a broad-based political party whose membership transcended the AT&LU to include businessmen and professionals. Thus, after three decades of being an appendage of the AT&LU, the ALP had finally come into its own and a period of consolidation followed. However, Rowan Henry was tragically murdered by his gardener on 25 June 1975 before he had a chance to bring the full weight of his personality and reputation to bear on the ALP.

On 3 February 1976, Parliament was dissolved and General Elections were set for 18 February. There followed an intense period of campaigning with both the PLM and ALP confident of victory. During this campaign the ALP undertook to abolish personal income tax in the event of their election. This was obviously of great attraction to the electorate and in combination with some of the more unpopular actions of the PLM, the ALP became irresistible to a large group of people. Hence on 19 February, the ALP had won ten seats, the PLM five, the Barbuda seat went to an independent, and there was a tie in the constituency of St. Phillips North where the candidates were Reuben Harris for the ALP and Edison

*Eric Burton was Barbuda's representative in Parliament during the nation's bid for independence*

Lewis for the PLM. The Court later gave the seat to Reuben Harris upon examination of disputed ballots.

What was remarkable about the election, however, is that while the ALP won 11 seats it received only 49.0 per cent of the vote, a slightly lower share than the losing PLM's 49.9 per cent.

As Leader of the ALP, V C Bird became Premier and appointed the Chairman of the Party, Lester Bird, to the post of Deputy Premier. Vere Bird Jnr, the eldest of V C Bird's sons and partner with Lester in the law firm of Bird & Bird, also won a seat in the Elections. Thus, was born a charge of "the Bird dynasty" in Antiguan politics.

When the ALP returned to office in 1976, in an attempt to stave-off secessionist forces on Barbuda, one of its first legislative actions was to pass an Act of Parliament establishing the Barbuda Local Government Council and giving it broad powers to conduct the local affairs of Barbuda.

Barbuda and Antigua had always

*Vere C Bird Snr*
*Prime Minister*

*Lester B Bird*
*Deputy Prime Minister*
*Minister for External*
*Affairs, Economic*
*Development, Tourism*
*& Energy*

*Keith Ford*
*Attorney General*
*and Minister of*
*Legal Affairs*

*Christopher O'Mard*
*Minister of Health*

*Ernest E Williams*
*Minister of Works*
*Communications &*
*Public Utilities*

*John E St Luce*
*Minister of Finance*

*Adolphus Freeland*
*Minister of Labour*
*& Social Security*

*Vere Bird Jnr*
*Advisor to*
*Prime Minister*

*Joseph Myers*
*Minister of Local*
*Government*

*Donald C Christian*
*Minister in Ministry*
*of Education*

*Reuben Harris*
*Minister of Education,*
*Youth & Culture*

*Robin Yearwood*
*Minister of*
*Agriculture*

*Hilroy Humphries*
*Parliamentary*
*Secretary in Ministry of*
*Economic Development*
*& Tourism*

*Hugh C Marshall*
*Minister of*
*Information*

*Senator Lionel Hurst*
*Minister in Ministry*
*of Public Works*

*The Government at Independence*

*On 11 November 1981, Lester Bird delivered the first address to the United Nations
on behalf of the newly independent Antigua and Barbuda*

experienced an awkward relationship, which is perhaps best captured by a phrase in a memorandum submitted by the Parliamentary Representative of Barbuda, Mr Eric Burton to the British Secretary of State of Foreign and Commonwealth Affairs in 1980. He described the perception of Barbudans in relation to Antigua as a "subtle feeling of neglect, inferiority, frustration and suppression which pervades the mind of every Barbudan."

The prevailing attitudes, however, did not manifest themselves in division between the two communities until 1967, when McChesney George, the representative of Barbuda in the Legislature and Minister of the Antigua Government split away from his old friend, V C Bird, the Chief Minister of Antigua. George promoted the idea of secession among the Barbudans, stressing that the

community had been neglected by the Antiguan Government. On 8 and 9 December 1967, 25 policemen were sent from Antigua to Barbuda because V C Bird felt that George was "stirring up trouble". In 1968, George made a statement to the committee of 24 at the United Nations pressing a case for Barbuda's secession from Antigua. The Government was sufficiently concerned about the effects of McChesney George's activity to commission a study "on the development potential of the Island of Barbuda, with a view to realising that potential."

In a memorandum submitted to the British Government during the independence negotiations in December 1980, the Antigua Government stated that "the ALP Government began implementation of many of the recommendations of the (study) but could

*Tim Hector, Editor of the 'Outlet' newspaper*

*Baldwin Spencer, Leader of the Opposition since 1989*

not continue the programme since it lost the General Election in 1971."

George's secessionist activity did not find fertile ground immediately. This was demonstrable when he contested the Barbuda seat in the 1971 General Elections as an independent and was defeated by the PLM candidate, Claude Earl Francis, who was also a Barbudan. However, while the majority of Barbudans may have voted for Francis, George still had a vociferous following for his secessionist ideas and created enough discontent on the island to encourage the PLM Government to send police to Barbuda more than once. In a

dramatic presentation to the British Foreign Office, the Barbudan Parliamentary representative, Eric Burton, described the PLM Government's attitude to Barbuda as follows:

"They continued the policy of their predecessors by sending police to Barbuda under the slightest pretext and on one occasion used tear gas and rifle bullets on the islanders because they staged a peaceful demonstration against an oppressive, abusive and tyrannical warden, an Antiguan."

The Barbudans were greatly encouraged by the success of Anguilla in breaking away

*Members of the Cabinet of the First Associated State. (l-r) V.C. Bird, Premier, Lionel A. Hurst, Deputy Premier, and Ministers E.E. Williams, E.H. Lake and M. George*

*The press in Antigua and Barbuda*

*V.C. Bird, campaigner for Independence and first leader of the 'new' Antigua and Barbuda*

from the union of St Kitts-Nevis because it felt neglected by the Government in St Kitts. In 1971, after four years of agitation for secession, Anguilla returned to being a British Colony.

*Princess Margaret, as The Queen's representative, presents Vere Cornwall Bird with the constitutional instruments for Antigua and Barbuda on Independence Day, 1 November 1981*

With secessionist forces on the ascendency in Barbuda, Claude Earl Francis abandoned the PLM to be elected Parliamentary Representative of Barbuda as an independent. Meanwhile, the newly created Barbuda Council functioned as a voice of dissent for the secessionist Barbudans and became involved in petty disputes with the central Government. In February 1978, Claude Earl Francis died and in a subsequent by-election, Eric Burton was elected to replace him as Barbuda's Parliamentary Representative. He too supported the secessionist cause and it was on that ticket that he was re-elected in the April 1980 General Elections which had the independence of Antigua as its principal theme.

The accusations of Government neglect of Barbuda was addressed by the Antigua Government at the Independence negotiations in London in December 1980.

The Government pointed out that among the powers accorded to the Barbuda Council in 1976 was "the right to collect revenues generated locally, such as hotel taxes and commissions on sand mined on Barbuda, and to spend such revenues on programmes and projects for Barbuda." The Government also stated that the five-year period 1971-1976, the PLM administration spent a total of EC$1,271,500 on Barbuda while in the period 1976-1979, the ALP Government spent EC$2,309,000 and this sum did not include the cost of subsidising electricity or sending a medical team to Barbuda weekly. The Government concluded that on a per capita basis Antigua received only $8.00 more than was spent on Barbuda per capita over the period 1976-1979.

The Barbuda secessionists opposed independence for Antigua if Barbuda was expected to be a part of the State. In what was to become characteristic of their campaign the Barbudans dramatically announced that they "would prefer death to a union of any sort with Antigua" They repeatedly told the British High Commissioner that Barbudans wanted one of two things, either separate independence or reversion to British Colonial status as in the case of Anguilla. A most impressive campaign was mounted including lobbies at the British Parliament, the retention of a Queen's Counsel in London and much media coverage. Over time, they abandoned the idea of separate independence. Their population was 1,200 people and even to their most ardent supporters that independence could not be sustained.

The focus of Barbudan concern, therefore became separation from Antigua and a return to British Colonial status though, in his remarks at the opening of the 1980 Constitutional Conference in London on Independence for Antigua, Eric Burton stated, "we have been told that Her Majesty's Government desires no dependencies. In this event, we are prepared to go into full independence on our own."

It was obvious from the outset of the Constitutional Conference that the British Government was not going to facilitate secession by Barbuda. The Chairman of the Conference and head of the British Delegation, Mr Nicholas Ridley, stated: "What we must do - not in the spirit of antagonism and the past - is to try and find if there is a way which will be satisfactory to all to integrate the state of Antigua with the island of Barbuda."

The British had attracted widespread international criticism over Anguilla in 1971. Moreover, Britain was anxiously divesting itself of colonies which were a drain on British taxpayers' money. In these circumstances, the UK Government was determined that Barbuda should not be allowed to secede from Antigua, but they wanted a good face put on it. The Antigua Government was not even entertaining discussion on secession. In its memorandum on Barbuda, the Government stated clearly that "territorial integrity must be paramount to encouraging fragmentation and balkanisation of states."

The Conference devoted nine of its twenty-two plenary sessions to Barbuda alone. In addition there were a number of informal meetings on particular aspects of the issue in which Sir Richard Posnett, the alternate Chairman of the Conference, steered the Barbuda delegation away from secession and encouraged the Antigua Government delegation towards a greater devolution of authority to the Barbuda Council over Barbudan affairs.

In fact, the solution to the Barbuda issue was found by supreme British diplomacy in alternating between threatening the Barbudans with total abandonment if they persisted with secessionists demands, and cajoling the Antiguan Government into greater concessions. In the end, the matter

*Elder statesmen - V.C. Bird, in his eighties, meets with South Africa's President Nelson Mandela*

of secession was dropped altogether and, except for a proposal that an independent body, such as the Commonwealth Secretariat, should be invited to review the operation of the new arrangements, the Government agreed to the devolution of greater powers to the Barbuda Council than they already had under the 1976 Act.

While the Barbudans continued to express dissatisfaction with the outcome of the Conference, they did absolutely nothing in pursuance of secession. On 16 April 1981, the Government amended the 1976 Act giving the Council the powers offered at the London Conference and making the island virtually self-governing. The Act was signed by the Governor-General, Sir Wilfred Jacobs, on 7 May 1981. The powers of the Council go beyond those of any Local Government anywhere in the world and include responsibilities as follows:

a) to administer agriculture and forestry;
b) to administer public health, medical and sanitary facilities and services;
c) to administer and regulate the provision of electricity and water services and other public utilities;
d) to construct, improve and maintain roads;
e) to raise and collect revenue pursuant to the provisions of this Act to enable the Council to meet expenses necessarily incurred or to be incurred in the performance of its powers and functions under this sub-section except to the extent that financial provision may be made from time to time by Parliament.

The Council was also given the duties of "promoting hotel and tourist development in accordance with and subject to any law relating to the alienation of land, foreign investment or tax incentives"; and

125

administering fisheries. In other words, apart from the control of land and security forces on the island, the Barbuda Council was accorded full control. The extent of the devolution of power to the Council was described as "unprecedented in our experience" by the British Government, whose spokesman pointed out that there were two constitutional safeguards for these powers:

"First, no Bill to alter Section 123 of the independence constitution which relates to the Barbuda Council can receive assent without approval of both Houses of Parliament and of a two-thirds majority referendum. Secondly, no bill relating to the Barbuda Local Government Act, which defines the Council's powers, can be regarded as being passed until it receives the consent of the Barbuda Council. Amendment by the Senate must similarly receive the Council's consent before amendment."

Further, the Government wrote into the Independence Constitution, the right of the Barbuda Council to appoint a Senator to the Upper House of Parliament. For, two and a half years afterwards, the Barbuda Council did not exercise their right to appoint a member of the Senate of Parliament, but following the 1984 General Elections, Hilbourn Frank was nominated by the Council after he unsuccessfully challenged Eric Burton for the Barbuda seat. Barbuda had achieved influence not only over its own affairs, but also over national decision-making in the country. However, while talk of secession has virtually ended, relations between the Government and the Council remain volatile as each attempts to assert what it regards as its legitimate authority.

As a post script to the Barbuda secession episode it is worth noting that, at the 1980 Constitutional Conference in London, the Government had proposed that the name of the independent state should be "Antigua-Barbuda". It was McChesney George who insisted on "Antigua and Barbuda".

After the ALP's return to office in 1976, the economy of the country turned around. Between 1977 and 1979, the economy grew by an average of eight per cent. New hotels were constructed, manufacturing enterprises mushroomed and employment increased. The Government boasted of its achievements which included:

- an increase in earnings for tourism workers from EC$4 million in 1974 to EC$$9.6 million in 1979
- an improvement in bank deposits from EC$64 million in 1973 to EC$131 million in 1979
- a hike in civil servants salaries from EC$15 million in 1973 to EC$38 million in 1979; and
- an expansion of factories from five in 1973 to 17 in 1979.

Lester Bird put the issue of independence to a convention of the ALP in September 1978, and he advocated it forcefully. He said:

"We would make a mockery of all the rebellions of our forefathers who, either individually or collectively, recognized our inherent right to be free of the British; we would cast a stigma on our children and their children when they learn after years of leading the way to freedom, Antigua did not have the courage to tear itself away from Britain and proudly say... We are free, we are our own masters, we are an independent nation."

The response of the convention was overwhelmingly in support of Lester Bird's call for independence. In its manifesto for the 1980 general election, the ALP stated that it "will immediately seek independence." By the time of the elections, independence was virtually a non-issue. The ACLM declared in its

*The Hon. Lester Bird, Prime Minister of Antigua and Barbuda*

*The President and the Prime Minister - Lester Bird meets Nelson Mandela*

Manifesto that the "ACLM unreservedly supports national independence for Antigua and Barbuda" and the PLM said it "has the personnel and expertise to lead Antigua into independence and the PLM has the will to work for a united front to develop an independent Antigua."

Opposition to the ALP crumbled at the 1980 general election. The party won 13 of the 17 seats, with only three going to the PLM and Barbuda returning an independent candidate. Everyone regarded this as a clear manifestation of the support by the Antiguan people for independence from Britain. Eight months later, the Antigua and British Governments met - with representatives of the PLM and Barbuda present - at Lancaster House in London to decide the Constitution of an independent Antigua.

Apart from Barbuda, which was the most contentious issue, the matters for discussion at the Conference centred on a few of the clauses in the draft Constitution prepared by the Antigua Government. Although the PLM delegation had argued strongly for the inclusion of provisions with respect to the right to strike, the right to collective bargaining and the collection of union dues, they identified the "main failure of the Conference" as "the failure satisfactorily to resolve the Barbuda situation." Both the PLM and Barbuda delegates declined to sign the report despite the fact that they had

*Prime Minister Lester Bird at the Antigua Recreation Ground*

"participated throughout the Conference and in the preparation of the report."

In June 1981, the Government introduced the Antigua and Barbuda Constitution Order 1981 and on 31 July 1981, Her Majesty The Queen signed the Order at Buckingham Palace in London.

On 31 October 1981, Princess Margaret, as the Queen's Representative, handed over the instruments of independence to V C Bird, Premier of Antigua, before a crowd estimated as half the population.

At midnight, the Union Jack was lowered for the first time in 328 years. As Prime Minister, V C Bird spoke to the independent nation of Antigua and Barbuda, he said:

"The ultimate safeguard of independence is productivity. This nation, born again tonight must commit itself to work and to work hard. For if we fail to do so, the consequence of our failure will be dependence on a new master who will,

once again, dictate our policies and direct our affairs. We must not have struggled so long and with such fortitude to exchange one master for another."

In a telling exchange at the conclusion of his speech, Princess Margaret remarked to V C Bird that she had not realised that he had felt so passionately about the need to be free from Britain. V C Bird's reply was a polite but deafening silence.

On 1 November the Antiguan flag was raised for the first time. On the morning of 2 November 1981 at a joint session of the Senate and the House of Assembly, Princess Margaret delivered a speech from the Throne setting out the Government's policy for the new nation of Antigua and Barbuda. She said:

"Above all else the human rights and freedoms of the people of Antigua and Barbuda are held sacrosanct by my Government. The Constitution safeguards

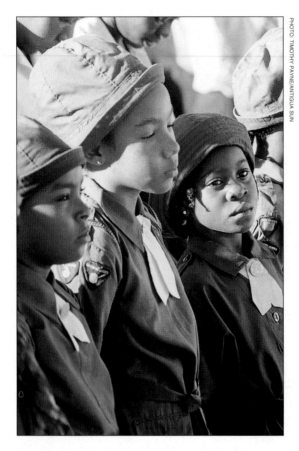

*Day of Remembrance, November 1998*

these rights particularly freedom of speech, of the press and of assembly. In ensuring that the Constitutional provisions are upheld, my Government will pay special attention to the rights of liberty, property, security and legal redress of grievances."

The new-born nation of Antigua and Barbuda was ready to embark on the adventure of full independence. Nine days later, on 11 November 1981, Antigua and Barbuda took its seat at the United Nations during the 36th General Assembly. Lester Bird, as Foreign Minister, made his country's international posture clear:

"My Country, Antigua and Barbuda, is a small State. We have no military muscle and want none, we have no quarrels with neighbours or nations further afield and we wish to keep it so. Our most earnest desire is a world secure in peace and stability; a world where man fulfils his obligation to the survival of his fellow man above the narrow concerns of ideology, above racial prejudice and above religious bigotry."

In the years after independence, the "challenge of the PLM - the only party ever to defeat the ALP - dissipated." In 1984, the PLM received only a minuscule vote and the ALP won all the Antigua seats. The lone opposition in parliament came from the independent Barbuda representative.

Opposition to the Government galvanized outside of parliament, principally in the Outlet Newspaper, an ACLM publication edited by Leonard Tim Hector, the party's leader. By the time of the 1989 election, the PLM had disintegrated and many of its former members with the support of the Antigua Workers Union formed the United National Democratic Party (UNDP) with a surgeon, Dr Ivor Heath, as its leader. The UNDP

*The armed forces are represented at the Remembrance Day Memorial Service*

*Acting Governor-General, Yvonne Maginley, Commander Elroy Thomas of the Antigua and Barbuda Defence Force and Prime Minister Lester Bird at the Remembrance Day Memorial Service*

performed creditably achieving 31 per cent of the votes, but securing only one seat in parliament. Shortly after, the opposition forces - UNDP and ACLM - decided to merge in order to try to wrest power from the ALP. The President of the AWU, Baldwin Spencer, was elected leader of the party.

As the end of the twentieth century approached and V C Bird reached his eighties, the ALP sought a new leader in 1992 - the first such attempt in 49 years. The contestants to replace V C Bird were Lester Bird and John E St Luce - the two men who had returned from their studies in England in 1968 to breathe new life into the ALP during its only period of opposition. When the result of the ballot by 300 delegates was announced at the ALP convention, no victor had emerged - Bird and St Luce had tied with 150 votes each.

A year passed before another convention was held. In September 1993,

Lester Bird defeated John E St Luce to become the second leader of the ALP in 50 years.

In March 1994, Lester Bird led the ALP to victory in general elections but with a decreased majority. The ALP secured 53% of the popular vote winning 11 seats while the opposition United Progressive Party got 43% of the vote nation-wide winning 5 seats. As usual, the Barbuda seat went to a Barbudan independent, Hilbourne Frank.

One of the major casualties of the ALP was Hugh Marshall Snr who lost his constituency of St Mary's South. In the September 1993 leadership contest, Marshall had thrown his hat into the ring to compete against Lester Bird and John E St Luce. In the end he had to withdraw for lack of support. Although Bird made Marshall a Senator in the Upper House of Parliament, Marshall resigned and tried to form his own political party which collapsed after a few months.

The ACLM, while keeping its separate identity with Tim Hector as its Leader, merged with the UPP for election purposes. No member of the ACLM won a seat in the elections, but Baldwin Spencer appointed Tim Hector as the Deputy Leader of the Party and a Senator. The elevation of Hector, despite his failure at the polls, maintained the fragile UPP. Its predecessor, the UNDP, had disintegrated after the 1989 elections.

The UPP vigorously opposed almost every move by the new government. They characterised the government's successful policy of attracting foreign investment as "giving away the country to foreigners", and they caused delays in the implementation of economic projects by taking the government and a major investor to Court, and by parliamentary action. In the event, the attempt at legal proceedings failed with the Courts rejecting the opposition case.

Nonetheless, one very large project by a Malaysian Investor, Dato Tan Kay Hock, costing in excess of US$200 million to build a tourist resort on Guiana Island and the nearby mainland area was considerably delayed depriving the economy of a significant injection of capital, employment and business opportunities.

Adding to these difficulties, the Lester Bird administration had to deal with two massive Hurricanes - Luis in September 1995 and Georges three years later. The estimate of damage caused by Hurricane Luis was US$500 million setting back the country's progress considerably as the Government had to pour money into rebuilding and rehabilitation rather than into new development. The national debt was also increased since, in the absence of international mechanisms to provide for post-disaster rehabilitation, the government had little choice but to borrow money on the commercial market at high rates of interest.

Despite these setbacks, Antigua and Barbuda's economy grew and its social conditions vastly improved during the Lester Bird administration. Except for 1995, the country experienced an average growth rate of 6% between 1994 and 1998 far higher than many industrialised nations. Its wages and salaries increased to almost US$8,000 per annum, ranking the country as having the second highest per capita income in the Eastern Caribbean surpassing larger territories such as Trinidad and Tobago and Jamaica. At the end of 1996, national savings amounted to US$150 million. The figure was higher than in any other country in the Eastern Caribbean. When it is considered that Antigua and Barbuda has one of the smallest populations of some 70,000 people, the totality of its national savings is even more impressive. Its gross capital formation at the end of 1996 was US$214 million with its closest rival in the Eastern Caribbean at US$114 million.

A further measure of how well the country performed under the Lester Bird administration is the amount of money spent on home construction. In 1996, US$58 million was spent on house construction, by 1997 the figure rose to US$93.3 million and by the end of 1998 it was estimated to reach a new high of US$118.5 million. Contrary to the argument that the country was being "given away to foreigners", 95% of the land in Antigua and Barbuda remained in the hands of the Government or nationals of Antigua and Barbuda in 1998. The remaining 5%, owned by foreigners, is mainly hotel resorts.

Despite the fact that throughout the period 1995 to 1997, Antigua and Barbuda gave refuge to over 3,000 Montserratians who had to flee their homeland after the eruption of the Soufriere Hills volcano, the unemployment rate in the country in mid-1998 was a mere 5%. By comparison, unemployment rates in other parts of the Caribbean were as high as 29%. Women were a principal beneficiary of the Lester Bird government. During the period 1994 to 1998, more women were employed than men, and women dominated the upper echelons of the public service as Permanents Secretaries, Speaker of the House, President of the Senate and Deputy Governor-General.

The rate of deaths among infants dropped dramatically as a result of improved health care and training, and life expectancy soared to an average age of 72 for men for 75 for women - as high as in the most developed countries of the world. Young people also witnessed improved conditions with government providing more scholarships for tertiary education, on a per capita basis, than all the countries of the Caribbean. Public sport facilities throughout the country were also improved and government support for athletes increased. By mid 1998, Antigua and Barbuda was enjoying the highest standard of living in its history.

These impressive social and economic conditions amid a contrastingly aggressive political climate led Lester Bird to say on 1st November, 1998 - the 17th Anniversary of Antigua and Barbuda's Independence:

"As we mark this 17th anniversary of our nation's independence in such advantageous circumstances, we should be mindful that freedom and prosperity are fragile plants. However beautiful their flowers might bloom or plentiful their fruits might bear, it takes but little to cause them to wither and die. It is up to us collectively as a nation and each of us individually to safeguard the gains we have made so far and to ensure our prospects for future success. It is up to us collectively as a nation and to each of us individually to fortify ourselves against the dangers to our independence and prosperity".

*Youth Rally 1998*

*Children from St Andrew's School at Youth Rally 1998*

PHOTO: TIMOTHY PAYNE/ANTIGUA SUN

*Youth Rally 1998 at the Antigua*
*Recreation Ground on 29 October*

*Pelicans rest on the remains of the old pier next to Heritage Quay in St John's Harbour*

*Fishing boats moored at the temporary jetty at Green Bay while a new fish landing facility is constructed at the old West Bus Station*

*The Catholic church of Our Lady of Perpetual Help in Tyrell's*

*St Paul's Anglican church in Liberta*

*The altar in the Catholic church
of Our Lady of Perpetual Help*

*Grace Bay Moravian church in Old Road village in St Mary's*

*Ebenezer Methodist Church*
*in St John's parish*

*Caves near Two Foot Bay on the north-east coast of Barbuda*

*Old wells such as this are still used in Barbuda to provide water for livestock*

*The ruins of the Codrington family beach house near Two Foot Bay, Barbuda*

*Members of the Antigua and Barbuda Police Force*

*Postmistress, teacher, farmer
and foster mother, Miss Warner
of Bendals village in the parish
of St John's, pictured with three
of her foster children, Vivian,
Trevor and Natasha*

*The ruins of the Royal Artillery quarters in Fort Shirley at Shirley Heights*

*A restored windmill on the Betty's Hope Plantation stands as a testament to the days of sugar and slavery*

*The Antigua and
Barbuda Museum
situated in the capital*

*A monument to honour national hero,
Prince Klaas, a slave who started a
rebellion to set his people free. He was
captured, tortured and killed in 1736*

*The Macumba Café in Willikies is owned and operated by members of the local community*

*The Antigua Brewery is the home of 'Wadadli' beer*

*'Liberta', the Antigua and Barbuda Coastguard launch*

*The marina at the Antigua Yacht
Club in Falmouth Harbour*

*The new Vendor's Mall under construction
at Lower Redcliffe and Thames Streets*

*Residential area at Galley Bay*

*Construction of the new fish landing and processing facility at the former West Bus Station. This project is a collaboration between the governments of Antigua and Barbuda and Japan*

*The Tindall Temple of the Seventh Day Adventists situated in Hut Grove in St John's*

*Hillside homes in Crosbies in the parish of St John's*

*A brightly decorated standpipe area in Parham*

*National Kite Flying Day*

*The 'Kite Hospital'*

*Feeding the flyers*

*'Welcome' to V.C. Bird International Airport*

*A tropical garden on the airport's observation deck*

*A decorative fountain greets visitors*

167

*The Virgin Atlantic inaugural flight touches down at V.C. Bird International Airport*

*Minister of Tourism, Rodney Williams (right) welcomes the Virgin Atlantic flight and the airline's representative*

*Air France Concorde arrives at V.C. Bird International Airport*

*Residential area in Crosbies*

*The parish church in St Phillip was established in 1830*

*The Jolly Harbour Marina and Shopping Complex at Bolans in St Mary's*

*Charcoal seller at the market*

*The market is an ideal meeting place*

*Stall traders can be found throughout St John's*

*Clayton Isaac sells his plants in the capital*

*Cottage industry is flourishing
in Antigua and Barbuda*

*Out and about in the city*

*Elder citizens present a united front*

*A small local tavern
in Parham village*

*St Peter's Anglican Church in
Parham village was built in 1840*

*The construction of a duty free extension at Historic Redcliffe Quay*

*New houses, such as this one in Fitches Creek, are being built to preserve Caribbean style*

*The first day of term at the Holy Trinity School in Codrington*

*St John's Cathedral*

*St John's Cathedral, as seen from Michael's Mount, stands proudly in the centre of the capital*

*The city centre*

*Rush hour!*

*Off to work*

*Lunch break*

*The bustling capital*

*The residence of the Governor-General located in St John's*

*Simon and Jimmy are tour guides for Estate Safari Jeep Tours*

*The Antigua Cub Scouts*

*The Antigua and Barbuda Fire Service on call-out*

*Sunset Cove Hotel in Runaway Bay*

*Sandals Antigua*

*'Cavalier', the rum of Antigua and Barbuda*

*'Time out' at the YMCA Sports Complex*

*Volleyball at the YMCA Sports Complex*

*Youngsters practice their skills*

*A training session for the Antigua and Barbuda National Cricket Team at the Antigua Sugar Factory*

*Locally known as the "Benna Boys", the team is pictured preparing for the 1998 Commonwealth Games*

*Former West Indies cricket captain, Viv Richards is the team's technical advisor*

*St John's as seen from
Michael's Mount*

*Independence Day celebrations, November 1998*

*The Hibiscus Residence is the first phase of the Friar's Hill Housing Development*

*Our Lady of the Valley
Anglican Church seen from
Valley Church Beach*

*Seatons village in St Phillip*

*Built in 1687, St George's Anglican Church at Fitches Creek was designated as a 'parish church' in 1725*

*A friendly village welcome*

*St Stephen's Anglican
Church in Glanvilles*

*Heritage Quay*

*Cedar Valley Springs residential area*

*The Bank of Antigua on
Airport Road in Coolidge*

*Construction of the new Antigua and Barbuda Hospitality Training Institute*

*The locally owned Big Banana Holding Company Restaurant at V.C. Bird international Airport*

*Minister Rodney Williams talking to the press on the site of the Antigua and Barbuda Hospitality Training Institute*

*Construction of a new fish landing and processing facility*

*The Antigua Distillery, where the local
Cavalier Rum is produced*

*New homes in the Cedar Valley area*

*Construction of a new
pharmacy building for the
Medical Benefits Scheme*

*The national costume*

*Locally produced hand-made goods*

*This bust of former Prime Minister V.C. Bird was produced in 1987 and is situated in front of the General Post Office in St John's*

*Construction of the George Piggott Courtyard Development at Redcliffe and Market Streets*

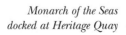

*Monarch of the Seas docked at Heritage Quay*

*St John's overlooking*
*Heritage Quay*

*George Ryan Building in Newgate Street, St John's*

# CHAPTER TEN

# *Investing in Paradise*

Antigua and Barbuda is a paradise for the business investor. Along with its year-round tropical climate, the country has a long tradition of political stability based on parliamentary democracy.

The government and the ruling Antigua Labour Party are committed to upholding the principle of free enterprise, a pledge shared by the main political parties. Successive governments have always respected the agreements and commitments made between previous administrations and investors.

While the government intervenes in the economy as a regulator in some instances, the private sector is the dominant force in the economy.

No investor has ever had assets nationalised or been forced to leave the island. Under the country's constitution, property can only be nationalised in exceptional circumstances, and even in such cases the law demands that fair compensation must be determined by an independent authority and must be paid promptly. This constitutional requirement is unusual in developing countries and makes Antigua and Barbuda a very attractive prospect for investment.

## Investment Protection Treaties

As an example of Antigua and Barbuda's commitment to protecting foreign investors in the country, the government has signed Bilateral Investment Protection Treaties with the governments of the United Kingdom and the Federal Republic of Germany. Under these Treaties, investors are afforded full protection with the strength of their governments behind them. The Treaties prohibit nationalisation without prompt and just compensation at market prices and grant investors treatment similar to that accorded to nationals.

## The Economy

The economy is small and open. Therefore, the country is subject to the vagaries of the economic conditions in countries from which it imports goods and services. To some extent, the effect of imported prices on the economy is moderated because the country's official currency - the Eastern Caribbean (EC) Dollar - enjoys a fixed exchange rate with the United States Dollar (US$1.00 = EC$2.70). The EC dollar is the strongest of all the Caribbean currencies and is used throughout the Leeward and Windward Islands.

The external debt of the country has grown rapidly in recent years and is due, largely, to the efforts made by certain government agencies to develop the country's infrastructure. Tourism remains the largest contributor to Gross Domestic Product (GDP). Agriculture and fisheries have reduced from 40 per cent of GDP in the 1960s, to about 12 per cent. Current

*Heritage Quay duty free shopping complex seen from the roof of the Heritage Hotel*

*The General Insurance Building on Upper Redcliffe Street*

manufacturing industries, which thrived in the 1980s, are export-orientated and involve the production of garments, paint, furniture, bedding and galvanized sheets.

## Communication

Air traffic to Antigua and Barbuda is served by V C Bird International Airport and accommodates all passenger and cargo aircraft. Among the many international airlines that operate regular flights to and from the country are British Airways, BWIA International, Air Canada, American Airlines, Air Jamaica, Condor, Air France and LIAT. Flying times are; Miami 3 hours, New York 4 hours, Toronto 4$^1$/$_2$ hours, London 8 hours, Paris 8 hours, Frankfurt 9$^1$/$_2$ hours, Zurich 9$^1$/$_2$ hours, Milan 9$^1$/$_2$ hours.

Antigua's busy sea port provides a good link to North America, Europe and the Far East. The container handling facilities are modern and efficient, and cater for roll-on/roll-off and lift-on/lift-off cargo. Several major shipping companies already use this port.

## Telecommunications

Antigua and Barbuda has an excellent telecommunications service. The British company, Cable and Wireless provides an international direct-dialling telephone service as well as telex, fax and data service, including e-mail and international databases to Europe, North America and other parts of the Caribbean.

## Industrial relations

Strong links exist between trade unions and political parties. This symbiotic relationship results in a favourable industrial climate. In 1975, a Labour Code was introduced to govern industrial relations, and an Industrial Court exists to settle disputes.

The country has a shortage of skilled labour, therefore, the government has a policy of granting work permits to employees of companies that need to import labour.

## Lifestyle

The setting-up of a business in Antigua and Barbuda comes with lifestyle benefits as

*Construction of the George Piggott Courtyard Development on Redcliffe and Market Streets purpose built for offices and shops*

well as those of a financial nature. Accommodation is comparable with Los Angeles, Florida or the suburbs of London, and numerous facilities are available, such as world-class golf courses, tennis courts, a wide variety of water sports and, of course, hundreds of beautiful beaches. Cable television provides access to many US channels, 24-hours-a-day.

Excellent schools up to secondary education level are also available.

## Financial institutions

A number of International banking institutions have branches in Antigua, including Barclays Bank, Royal Bank of Canada, Bank of Nova Scotia and the Canadian Imperial Bank of Commerce, the Bank of Antigua and the Swiss American National Bank of Antigua which has the most branches in the country. There are also two locally-owned banks - Antigua Commercial Bank and Antigua and Barbuda Investment Bank.

A number of local and international insurance companies offer a wide range of insurance services.

## Doing business in Antigua and Barbuda

There are four principal means of doing business in the country:
1. Sole Proprietorship
2. Partnership
3. Branch of foreign corporations
4. Company - public or private

## No Personal Income Tax

One of the characteristics that helps to make Antigua and Barbuda a paradise for business and investment, is that it levies no personal income tax.

Corporation Tax is imposed at a flat-rate of 40 per cent on profits, and double taxation treaties are in force with the United Kingdom, Canada and the United States with regard to income earned in Antigua and Barbuda.

A property tax of 10 per cent of the annual rental value of the property is payable annually by citizens of Antigua and Barbuda. Non-citizens pay 20 per cent.

Duty is payable for the export of lobsters, sea island cotton and sugar. The government does not impose export duties on any other items.

## Incentives for investors

The legal basis for Antigua and Barbuda's 'tax holidays' for investors is codified in the Fiscal Incentives Act. The length of the 'holiday' depends on the amount of value added in Antigua and Barbuda. The definition of local value added is the amount realised from the sales of the product over a continuous period of twelve months, minus the following:

a. The cost of imported raw materials, components, parts of components, fuels and services;
b. Wages and salaries paid to foreign nationals;
c. Profits and dividends distributed to foreign nationals;
d. Interest, management charges and other income payments to non-residents, including companies;
e. Depreciation of imports of plant, machinery and equipment.

The government offers numerous concessions to investors, particularly if the investment is substantial. Typical concessions include:

- Freedom from payment of Corporate Tax on the profits arising out of the profitable operations of the company for a period of fifteen years in the first instance which is eligible for renewal for a further fifteen years
- The waiving of all Import Duties and Consumption Tax on the importation of materials and equipment used in the operation of the company
- A grant of an Export Allowance in the form of an Extended Tax Holiday on the exportation of goods produced in Antigua and Barbuda
- The right to repatriate all capital royalties, dividends and profits free of all taxes or any other charges on foreign exchange transactions

In addition, the government allows a company to import a standby electricity generator free of all import duties and consumption taxes. All office equipment and vehicles to be used in the company's operations can be imported free of duty and consumption taxes. The government grants all work permits and the necessary residential status to all expatriates who are key personnel in the operations of a company.

## Off-shore banks and companies

In 1982, the government introduced the International Business Corporations Act permitting off-shore banking, insurance and trust corporations. The Act was amended in 1998. It provides for:

- Full tax exemption
- No control on exchange and freedom to operate bank accounts anywhere
- No minimum capital requirement, except for:
  *i.* Banking, where US$5 million is required together with the filing of quarterly returns;
  *ii.* Trusts, where a minimum capital requirement of US$500,000 and the filing of quarterly returns
  *iii.* Insurance Companies, which must file annual reports and have a reserve capital of US$250,000.
- Fifty-year guarantee of Tax-Free Status

The formation of an off-shore company costs US$250 and is renewable every year.

## Duty-free access to large markets

Tourism is the major industry in Antigua and Barbuda, and with 365 beaches in the country, plenty of scope remains for foreign investment. Foreign-owned hotels should have a minimum of fifty rooms.

Antigua and Barbuda enjoys duty-free access for a number of goods into the markets of the European Union, Canada, the United States, Venezuela and eleven Caribbean countries. This access, when combined with the generous incentives offered by the government, makes Antigua and Barbuda an investors' paradise.

*Heritage Quay offers shopping and dining*

*The Bencorp Office Building on the corner of High Street and Independence Drive is the home of both the Benjies Business Centre and the main branch of the Swiss American National Bank*

*Deluxe rooms at*
*Sandals Antigua*

*The new State Insurance office complex, located at Thames and Long Streets in St John's*

*The Bank of Antigua*

*The cruise ship Monarch of the Seas is a majestic sight in Heritage Quay*

*The offices of Stanford Development Company in Coolidge*

*A collaboration between the governments of Antigua and Barbuda and Japan has led to the construction of the former West Bus Station into a new fish landing and processing facility*

*Founded by rock musician Eric Clapton, who has had a home in Antigua since the early eighties, the Crossroads Centre at Willoughby Bay is a drugs and alcohol rehabilitation centre*

*Justin Simon Building in Newgate Street, St John's, is the chambers of Simon, Fuller & Co. Attorneys At Law*

*Multi-purpose centre at Perry Bay*

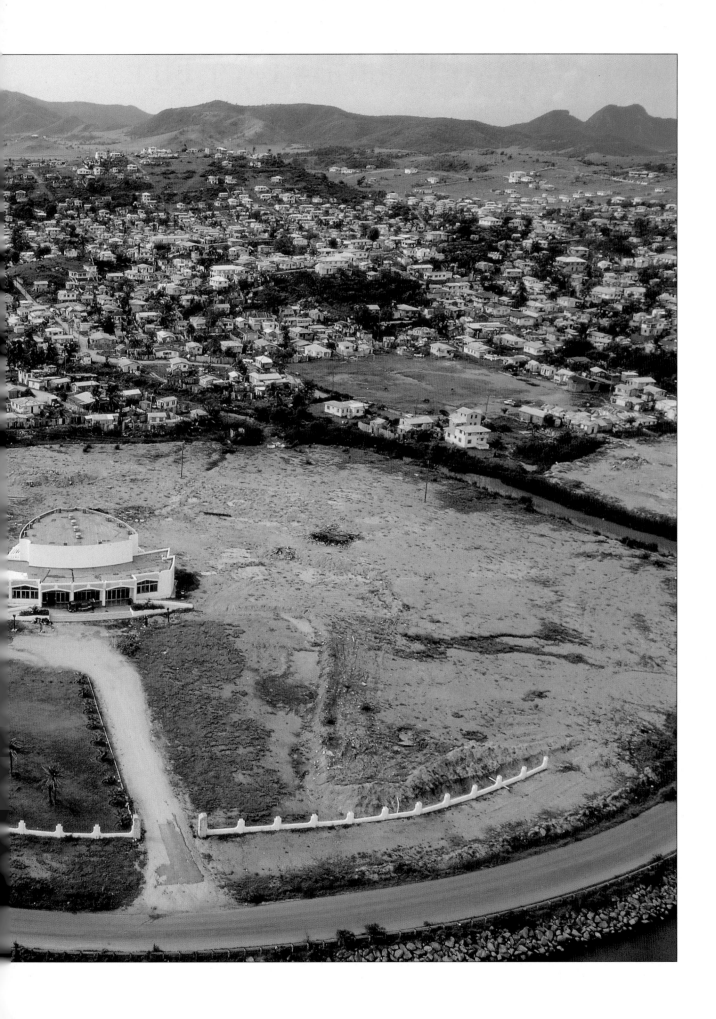

# ANTIGUA AND BARBUDA FACT FILE

■ Antigua and Barbuda is a twin-island state whose territory includes a handful of small islands - Redonda (the largest and uninhabited), Long Island, Guiana Island, Green Island, Crump Island and Pelican Island.

■ Antigua is 108 square miles (280 sq km), Barbuda, which is 32 miles north, is 62 sq miles (160 sq km), and Redonda, which is twenty miles to the north-west, is a little over half a square mile (1.6 sq km).

■ The land mass of Antigua consists of volcanic rock, which occupies 40-45%, and the rest is formed from sedimentary rocks, mainly limestone. The foundation of Barbuda is made of limestone.

■ Antigua can be divided into three principal regions; a 'high' region consisting of precipitous hills of volcanic rock, the highest point being Boggy Peak which stands at just over 1,300 feet; a rolling lowland area known as the Central Plain which runs from the capital, St John's, in the north-west, to the spectacular Willoughby Bay in the south-east, and occupies about twenty square miles; and a limestone area between the hills and the plain.

■ Antigua's coastline stretches for more than ninety miles and consists of hundreds of beaches, coves and bays, many with fine white sand. There are also extensive coral reefs which not only maintain magnificent marine life, but also protect the coast from erosion and provide calm waters in the bays.

■ The islands receive little rainfall - an average of 45 inches a year - and it is not uncommon for there to be no rainfall in some years.

■ Barbuda has a very flat landscape except for a small area which rises to approximately 128 ft called 'The Highlands'.

■ The island is renowned for its beaches, some of which are regarded as the most beautiful and spectacular in the Caribbean. Almost the entire coastline is edged with coral reefs.

■ The majority of Antiguans and Barbudans have never seen the nation's third largest island, Redonda, which is isolated and rocky. Just one mile long and less than half-a-mile wide, the landscape rises to one thousand feet with steep cliffs on all sides.

■ On 10 November 1493, the day before Christopher Columbus sailed past Antigua, the intrepid explorer named the rocky out-crop, Santa Maria la Redonda. However, the island was hardly ever used and remains strictly for the birds.

■ The population of Antigua is approximately 72,000 and Barbuda has a little over 1,200 residents. However, the census carried out in 1981 revealed a population in Antigua and Barbuda of 78,000 and 1,500 respectively. The recent decline is due, largely, to emigration to the United States.

■ Ninety-one percent of the people of Antigua and Barbuda are of African descent whose ancestors were brought to the islands as slaves in the 17th and 18th centuries from the west coast of Africa.

■ The remaining population is made up of people of Lebanese and Syrian descent whose ancestors came as traders at the beginning of the twentieth century; the descendants of Portuguese labourers who fled from Madeira during a famine in the mid-1800s; North Americans and Canadians who settled throughout the twentieth century; and other Caribbean nationals, mainly from Dominica, Montserrat, St Kitts, Guyana, Jamaica and the Dominican Republic.

■ In recent years, small numbers of Chinese nationals have been drawn to Antigua and Barbuda to work in the garment manufacturing and restaurant industry.

■ The political structure of the country is firmly based on the British system of parliamentary democracy. Elections are held at least every five years and they are contested by several political parties throughout the country's seventeen constituencies.

■ The State system comprises the Government, Parliament, Judiciary and the Head of State.

■ Antigua and Barbuda's Head of State is Queen Elizabeth II.

# USEFUL INFORMATION

## GETTING THERE

**By Air:** Most visitors to Antigua arrive by air at V C Bird International Airport, located on the northeast corner of the island. Flights arrive daily from the United States and Europe. LIAT airlines - whose headquarters are located in Antigua - provides scheduled air services throughout the Caribbean and South America.

**By Sea:** Cruise ships that visit regularly, dock in Deep Water Harbour at Heritage Quay in the capital, St John's. For those travelling by boat points of entry are St John's on the west coast, English Harbour or the St James's Club on the southern shore, or Crabbs Marina on the northeast coast.

Antigua and Barbuda is located in the middle of the Leeward Islands in the Eastern Caribbean, approximately 17 degrees north of the equator and 1,200 miles southeast of Miami. Barbuda lies 30 miles north of Antigua.

## ENTRY

Proof of citizenship is required for entry - a passport, birth certificate, or voter's card is best - as well as a return or onward ticket. Upon leaving Antigua, a departure tax of EC$50 (US$20) is payable if you have been in Antigua for more than 24-hours.

## CURRENCY

The currency used in Antigua and Barbuda is the Eastern Caribbean (EC) Dollar. Credit cards and travellers' cheques are accepted almost everywhere (except for some small shops and restaurants), as well as United States Dollars. The exchange rate for US dollars is generally lower at hotels and restaurants than at the banks.

## BANKS

Normal banking hours are 8am to 2pm Monday to Thursday, and 8am to 4pm on Friday.

## LOCAL TAX

A 10% service charge is added to all accounts in lieu of gratuities, as well as 8.5% government tax.

## CLIMATE

Temperatures range from the mid-seventies to the mid-eighties Fahrenheit, with higher temperatures in the summer months. Rainfall is very low and averages about 45 inches per year - so water is always considered precious. The rainy months are September, October and November.

## TIME ZONE

GMT (Greenwich Mean Time) minus 4 hrs.

EST (Eastern Standard Time) plus 1 hr.

## ELECTRICITY

Electricity supply is either 110 or 220 volt. Most hotels use 110 volt. Please check before using appliances.

## WATER

Tap water is safe to drink at hotels and throughout the island bottled water is readily available.

## COMMUNICATIONS

Antigua has modern telephone, telex, and cable facilities that provide 24-hour communications world-wide. AT&T has installed a 'USA Direct' service at the airport and a number of other locations. Cable and Wireless can connect credit card, phonecard, and collect calls to any location. Most hotels now offer fax facilities.

## LANGUAGE

English.

## POST OFFICE

The central post office is located in the capital at the intersection of Long and Thames Streets. A post office is also situated at the airport.

## HEALTHCARE

There are excellent physicians in Antigua and Barbuda, and there are three hospitals - two in Antigua and one in Barbuda. Construction of a new hospital is under way

## SHOPPING

Store opening hours vary. Most shops in St John's and the Jolly Harbour Shopping Centre are open from 9am to 5pm, Monday to Saturday. In the

Heritage and Redcliffe Quay duty-free areas, many stores open on Sundays when a cruise ship is in port.

## CHURCH SERVICES

Antigua has more than one hundred churches, representing Anglicans, Roman Catholics, Moravian, Seventh Day Adventists, Jehovah's Witnesses, and Methodists. Information about church services is available at most hotels.

## NATIONAL AND PUBLIC HOLIDAYS

Most shops, banks and government offices are usually closed on these dates:

- New Year's Day (January 1)
- Good Friday
- Easter Monday
- Labour Day (first Monday in May)
- Whit Monday
- Queen's Official Birthday (second Saturday in June)
- Carnival Monday (first Monday in August)
- Carnival Tuesday (the first Tuesday in August)
- Merchants Holiday (first Monday in October. Banks and government offices remain open)
- Independence Day (November 1)
- Christmas Day (December 25)
- Boxing Day (December 26)

## GETTING ABOUT

### Bicycles (for rent)
Many villages, historic churchyards and secluded coves are only accessible via unpaved roads, making cycling a popular mode of transport.

### Buses
Antigua does not have an official bus service and there are no numbered routes, no designated stops or scheduled departures.

However, there are many enterprising individuals who run their own 'buses' (usually small vans and mini-buses) which operate sporadic services from 5.30am until nightfall. Most journeys connect the capital, St John's, with the outlying districts of the island.

These services, while irregular, offer a clean, safe and inexpensive way to see areas of Antigua usually missed by most visitors. Ensure that you agree a bus fare with the driver prior to departure.

### Driving
You are required by law to obtain a temporary 90-day Antigua Driver's License before driving in Antigua and Barbuda. This may be obtained either through a car rental agency or at a police station. To qualify, you must hold a valid driver's licence issued in your country of origin. A fee will be charged.

Antigua follows the British system of driving (drive on the left).

Most filling/gas stations will accept either US or EC dollars.

The national speed limit is 40 miles per hour, except in the capital, St John's, and in the villages, where the speed limit is 20 miles per hour.

### Car Rental
The rental of a car or a four-wheel drive vehicle is the most popular means to getting around Antigua, and there are many car rental companies to choose from.

### Taxis
First-time visitors to Antigua and Barbuda may feel more comfortable travelling by cab. Most taxis are individually owned and belong to an association that controls their rates. Hotels usually display standard rates to the popular tourist destinations and sights.

Trying to hail a taxi on the street may prove unsuccessful. It is advisable to arrange taxi transport through your hotel or guest house.

Confirm the fare with the driver before departure and be certain to establish if payment should be made in US or EC Dollars. If your trip takes you to some remote region, be sure to arrange in advance for return transportation.

### Sea Excursions
Most of the more popular attractions are located in coastal regions, and the offshore approach can add an exciting alternative to the conventional. There are many organised sea tours, some of which include deep-sea fishing, scuba-diving, dining and dancing.

### Tours
The easiest way to see Antigua and Barbuda is to join an organised sightseeing tour. Almost every hotel offers at least one, usually lasting between three and four hours.

## SIGHTSEEING IN ANTIGUA

**Anglican Cathedral of St John the Divine:** The twin spires of this magnificent cathedral dominate the capital's skyline. Known as St John's Cathedral, the building was constructed as a church in 1681, and then re-built in 1722. It played an active part in the island's life, and was used in 1805 for the investiture of Admiral Hood by Lord Lavington. Just as pleas were being made for the church to be elevated to the status of cathedral, the great earthquake struck in 1843. Re-building followed and the cathedral was consecrated in 1848. The interior is encased in wood in order to protect it from both hurricane and earthquake damage. This was put to good use when another earthquake struck in 1974. It is an architecturally unusual and interesting building comprising two towers in a baroque style. The graveyard contains some headstones that are more than 300-years-old.

**Antigua and Barbuda Archives:** This is a repository for historic documents and a display centre of the country's history.

**Antigua Recreation Ground:** This is a modern venue for Caribbean and international cricket and football matches. Antiguans have watched many of their native sons - including legendary cricketers Viv Richards and Richie Richardson - playing and leading the West Indies Cricket Team to victory.

**Betty's Hope Sugar Plantation:** Established by Christopher Codrington in 1674, this sugar plantation was the nucleus to all of Antigua's sugar production and slave labour.

**Clarence House:** Constructed in 1787, this graceful Georgian house overlooks Nelson's Dockyard. It was built for Prince William Henry, the then Duke of Clarence, and Captain of HMS Pegasus, who later became King William IV in 1830. The house was later occupied by the Commissioner of the Dockyard and Governors of the island. Princess Margaret stayed there for a short visit during her honeymoon in 1960. Clarence House is still used on special occasions by Britain's Royal Family and is open to the public.

**Devil's Bridge:** At the end of the road to Long Bay at Indian Town Point is Devil's Bridge, a natural limestone arch created by wave erosion.

**Dickenson Bay:** Over one mile long, Dickenson Bay, on the northwest coast, is the most popular tourist beach. With many hotels, restaurants and beach activities and water sports, this area is a major attraction.

**Dow's Hill Interpretation Centre:** This is a perfect vantage point from where visitors may see the whole of Nelson's Dockyard. Also within the Dow`s Hill area is a bat cave which, according to folklore, was used as a hide-out by escaped slaves.

**English Harbour:** Situated in an ancient volcano cone, English Harbour is made up of virtually land-locked basins with only a narrow passage to the sea - this provided natural protection both from the elements and from sightings from the sea. An active yachting centre as well as historic attraction, the harbour was developed into a naval dockyard by the British.

**Falmouth Harbour:** For hundreds of years, Falmouth Harbour has been a safe anchorage for ships. It is very much in use today, providing moorings and facilities for sailing and motor yachts alike.

**Fig Tree Drive:** In contrast to the sandy beaches of Antigua is Fig Tree Drive, a road from the town of Liberta to Old Road at the head of Carlisle Bay. Winding its way through lush vegetation and rainforest, the road is sometimes engulfed beneath the green canopy. Fig Tree Drive is the most thickly wooded area of Antigua and an indication of the island's terrain before the land was shorn of its trees and vegetation to make way for the sugar cane fields.

**Fort Barrington:** Situated on the northern side of Deep Bay, this fort was built on top of Goat Hill around 1779. Of all of the forts in Antigua, this one witnessed the most military combat. The fortress was named in honour of the British admiral who had captured St Lucia from the French. Now in ruins, the fort served as a signal station until 1960.

**Fort Berkeley:** Built in three stages between 1704 and 1755, Fort Berkeley, with its twenty-nine cannons, was the island's main defense.

**Fort Charles:** One of the oldest forts in Antigua, Fort Charles can be found on Blake Island in Falmouth Harbour. Constructed in 1672, the fort once boasted fourteen guns to defend Falmouth.

**Fort George:** A handful of ruins is all that remains of Fort George situated on Monk's Hill, where once stone walls encircled the seven-acre site.

**Fort James:** Standing at the northern entrance to St John's Harbour is Fort James. It was built in 1675 and later rebuilt in 1749. At the time of the American Revolution, there were 36 cannons in place and accommodation for seventy men. Throughout the 19th century, a gun was fired at sunrise and at sunset, and salutes were fired for visiting warships. Twelve men were required to operate each gun. Ten cannons remain, each weighing over two tons which, when in use, had a firing range of nearly two miles.

**Fort Shirley:** See Shirley Heights

**Half Moon Bay:** Considered by many Antiguans to be the most beautiful beach on the island. The circular shape of the bay with its entrance facing the Atlantic Ocean combine to create a wide variety of surf conditions.

**Harmony Hall:** Located on the east coast near Nonsuch Bay, Harmony Hall was built around an old sugar mill. This complex comprises a restaurant and bar and an art gallery with paintings, photographs, and arts and crafts by local artists. An annual crafts fair held in November.

**Museum of Marine and Living Art:** Located on Gambles Terrace, the museum contains relics from ancient shipwrecks, historical photographs and articles, a collection of local seashells, and samples of the many types of sand found throughout the islands.

**Nelson's Dockyard:** First developed in 1743, Nelson's Dockyard has now become a National Park. Its ancient buildings have been carefully restored and turned into shops, inns and restaurants. The dockyard is the focal point for Antigua Sailing Week. There is a small museum housed in an elegant two-storey building known as The Admiral's House.

**Old Court House:** The oldest building in St John's is the Old Court House at the corner of Long and Market Streets which houses the Museum of Antigua and Barbuda. The building was built of freestone from Long Island, Guiana Island and Pelican Island in 1747. It was severely damaged by the great earthquake of 1843 and later restored. Apart from the usual court house functions, the building was also used to host balls, dinners, bible meetings and charity sales. It was damaged again by an earthquake in 1974, and reconstructed in the early 1980s.

**Parham Church:** This is the local name given to St Peter's Anglican Church in the village of Parham. It has been referred to as, "the finest church in the British West Indies". First built around 1700 - and re-built in the 1840s after the original wooden structure had burnt down - it was designed by the English architect, Thomas Weeks. Its unique, octagonal shape makes it one of the most distinctive and attractive churches in the Caribbean.

**Prison:** Originally constructed in 1735 as a barracks for the 38th Foot Regiment, which was stationed in Antigua from 1707 to 1764, the building was converted into a prison in 1831.

**Redcliffe Quay:** Located in lower Redcliffe Street is Redcliffe Quay, a shopping complex which has been carefully restored to its original style.

**Shirley Heights:** It was to defend the naturally strategic location of English Harbour that fortifications were built at Shirley Heights between 1780 and 1790. Fort Shirley was situated on the overhanging mountain ridges by order of General Thomas Shirley when he became Captain General and Governor-in-Chief of the Leeward Islands. Now in ruins, this was once a very large fortification which currently houses a small museum. The blockhouse consists of barracks and stables, and cannon platforms set on the 400 feet high Cape Shirley, a magnificent lookout point. There is a restaurant called 'The Lookout' from where there are spectacular views of English Harbour, Nelson's Dockyard and Falmouth Harbour. Every Sunday, Shirley Heights is the island's favourite meeting point. With a party atmosphere, barbecue and steelband music, this is an event not to be missed.

**St George's Anglican Church:** Situated at Fitches Creek, this was built in 1867 and then remodelled fifty years later.

**St John's:** The capital city, St John`s is one of the oldest trading ports in the Caribbean and dates back to the early 17th century. No vacation is complete without visiting this busy city. The original town was built around a fort whose construction began on Rat Island in 1672. A market was built in 1702 and cross streets were laid out with broad avenues running east and west. These avenues were joined by narrower north and south cross streets. The institutional buildings were put in place in the early 19th century; Government House in 1801 and a General Post Office in 1850. The mid-19th century witnessed a period of great construction activity in St John's following a fire in 1841 which devastated many of the original buildings. The result of different eras of construction has resulted in a rich blend of architectural styles - Georgian, Victorian and Romantic. The construction of a new vendors mall, fish market and general market place, is under way.

**Police Station:** The police station in St John's was built in 1754 on Market Street as a guard house and jail. Four years later an arsenal was added to provide a central place for the storage of munitions. In 1831, the jail was moved to the barracks in the east end of town, where it is today. Old bayonets were used to cap the railings of the courtyard when the militia was disbanded in 1838. The arsenal was used until the 1930s and Antigua's old records were kept in vaulted stone rooms which were once jail cells.

**St Peter's Anglican Church:** See Parham Church

## SIGHTSEEING IN BARBUDA

Just fifteen-minutes' flight from Antigua, is the sister island, Barbuda. With two exclusive resorts - the long-established Coco Point and the relatively new K Club - this truly spectacular island is often overlooked by tourists.

The immediate impact upon the visitor to Barbuda is the flatness of the island. The second, and most lasting impression is the incredible beauty and emptiness of the pink coral sand beaches and the colours of the surrounding sea.

Points of interests are the Frigate Bird Sanctuary, Codrington Village, Martello Tower and Fort, the Highlands, the caves and, of course, the many wonderful beaches. For the best view of the island it is advisable to take a guided tour and, remember, Barbuda gets very hot!

LIAT airlines operates scheduled daily flights to Barbuda and special day trips.

## ANTIGUA SAILING WEEK

Celebrated annually at the end of April, Antigua Sailing Week attracts more than three hundred of the world's finest sailing craft for a week of racing, and partying!

By 1967, the event's original organisers and the Antigua Hotels Association had joined forces and extended the event to three full days of racing.

This week-long spectacle, which is for sailing enthusiasts and party-goers alike, is one of the most renowned yachting events in the world.

## CARNIVAL

Antigua's carnival is often described as one of the Caribbean's most colourful and exciting summer festivals. With an explosion of artistic and cultural talent, music, steelbands and calypso, the streets come alive with parades, bands, troupes and a multitude of colourful costumes.

Held during the last week of July and culminating on the first Monday and Tuesday of August, this annual event attracts locals and visitors.

## EATING OUT (Local dishes)

**Conch Stew:** An excellent shellfish stew made with the meat of the large conch and cooked with onions, tomatoes and spices.

**Pepper Pot:** This is a rich delicious stew containing salt beef, pork, pumpkin, paw-paw (papaya), spinach, peas, aubergines and okras, with onion, garlic and spices. It can be served with dumplings or with a cornmeal pudding locally known as 'fungee'.

**Salt Fish:** This is the traditional Antiguan Sunday morning breakfast dish. It is dried cod which has been boiled, boned and cooked in a rich onion and tomato sauce. As a breakfast dish it is usually accompanied by 'doucouna', a small pudding made from grated sweet potato and coconut mixed with flour and spices and boiled in a banana leaf.

**Souse:** This is boiled pork marinated in water and lime-juice with onions, peppers, garlic and cucumber. It is served with lettuce and tomatoes and eaten with hot bread rolls.

## FURTHER INFORMATION

For more details about visiting Antigua and Barbuda, contact the Antigua and Barbuda tourism and information offices in the following countries:

### Antigua

Antigua and Barbuda Department of Tourism, PO Box 363, St John's. Tel: 268 462 0029/0480. Fax: 268 462 2483

Antigua Hotels & Tourist Association, PO Box 454, Lower St Mary's Street, St John's. Tel: 268 462 3703/0374. Fax: 268 462 3702. E-mail: ahta@candw.ag

### Canada

Antigua and Barbuda Department of Tourism & Trade, 60 St Clair Avenue East, Suite 304, Toronto, Ontario M4T 1N5. Tel: 416 961 3085. Fax: 416 961 7218. E-mail: info@antigua-barbuda-ca.com

### Germany

Antigua and Barbuda Department of Tourism, Thomasstrasse 11, D-61348 Bad Homburg. Tel: 06172 21504. Fax: 06172 21513

### France

Office du Tourisme D'Antigua et Barbuda, 43 Avenue de Priedland, Paris 75008. Tel: 053 75 15 71. Fax: 053 75 15 69

### Italy

Antigua and Barbuda Department of Tourism, Via S Maria Alla Porta, 9, 20123 Milan. Tel/Fax: 3902 87 79 83

### United Kingdom

Antigua and Barbuda Department of Tourism, Antigua House, 15 Thayer Street, London W1M 5DL. Tel: 0171 486 7073/4/5. Fax: 0171 486 1466. E-mail: antbar@msn.com

### United States

Antigua and Barbuda Department of Tourism & Trade, 610 Fifth Avenue, Suite 311, New York, NY 10020. Tel: 212 541 4117. Fax: 212 757 1607. E-mail: info@antigua-barbuda.org. Internet: www.interknowledge.com/antigua-barbuda

Antigua and Barbuda Consulate General, 25 SE 2nd Avenue, Suite 300, Miami, Florida 33131. Tel: 305 381 6762. Fax: 305 381 7908

Embassy of Antigua and Barbuda, 3216 New Mexico Avenue NW, Washington, DC 20016. Tel: 202 362 5122. Fax: 202 362 5225

# Morgen bright an

Wie eine pralle, riesige Orange steigt die Sonne langsam über der Karibik auf. Lichtstreifen - manche gelb, andere rot, wieder andere strahlendweiß - breiten sich auf dem Wasser aus und tanzen und schlängeln sich über die kleinen, sanften Wellen auf eine Küste zu, wo die zurückweichenden Schatten der Nacht beginnen, die Strände mit ihrem weißen und goldenen Sand nach und nach zu enthüllen. Der Tag bricht an auf Antigua und Barbuda, hier, wo jeder Tag ein Sommertag ist.

Während die Sonne langsam höher steigt, verwandelt sich ihr goldener Glanz mehr und mehr in eine atemberaubende Helligkeit, die sich über das Meer und das Land ergießt. Die Luft ist noch kühl und obgleich die Sonne begonnen hat, Herrschaft über die Erde zu ergreifen, ist sie noch zu jung, um die starken Passatwinde aus Nordosten zu durchdringen, die beständig über das Meer hinweg wehen.

Nach uralter Tradition schaukeln kleine Fischerboote über das Meer. Mit Fischen beladen für den morgendlichen Markt sind sie auf dem Heimweg zur Küste. Die Fischer ziehen bei Nacht hinaus. Sie wissen, dass die Fische bei Tagesanbruch an die Oberfläche gelockt werden, angezogen von den Strahlen der neugeborenen Sonne, ehe deren Hitze sie in die kühleren Gewässer unten am Meeresboden zurückdrängt. Das rhythmische Tuckern der kleinen Außenbordmotoren der Fischerboote vermischt sich mit dem lauteren Dröhnen von Jetskis, Motorbooten und Jachten, die für die Urlauber, die ja schließlich das meiste aus ihrem Karibikurlaub machen wollen, fertig gemacht werden.

Langsam werden auch die ersten Menschen auf Antigua und Barbuda sichtbar: zuerst ein paar junge Einheimische, die am Strand entlang joggen und gelegentlich ins Wasser eintauchen, um sich von dessen belebender Kraft erfrischen zu lassen. Auch Urlauber kommen zu dieser frühen Morgenstunde heraus und tauchen ein in die herrlichen Fluten. In Erfüllung eines lang gehegten Verlangens lassen sie sich auf dem Rücken treiben, mit entspannten Muskeln, während alle Spannung von ihnen abfällt und sie nur ihre Gesichter der kribbelnden Wärme der herrlichen Sonne zuwenden.

Auch Vögel gehören zu dem morgendlichen Treiben. Auf Antigua und Barbuda gibt es 140 verschiedene Vogelarten, von denen 90 regelmäßig zu sehen sind. Einige von ihnen sind Jäger - zum Beispiel die Meerespelikane, die über die Meeresoberfläche streichen und sich dann plötzlich ins Wasser stürzen, um nach ein paar Sekunden mit dem Frühstück im Schnabel wieder aufzutauchen. Andere flattern von Baum zu Baum, wo sie mit ihrem Gesang die Perfektion der Natur untermalen. Der Bananaquit und der Gimpel der Kleinen Antillen, schwarz oder

grau mit rötlicher Brust sind die am weitesten verbreiteten Vogelarten.

Während die Sonne höher steigt und das Land in ihrem Lichte badet, kommen mehr und mehr Farben zum Leben - die Blätter sind jetzt lebhaft grün, Blumen - Bougainvillea, Hibiskus und Oleander - erstrahlen in rot, gelb, weiß und violett. Kokos- und andere Palmen, die seit Jahrzehnten majestätisch die Küsten dieser Inseln einrahmen, erheben sich in den klaren, blauen Himmel, an dem nur hier und dort ein paar kleine, weiße Wölkchen schweben. Gelegentlich sieht man entweder eine sehr alte oder eine sehr junge Palme, die sich nach unten krümmt, aber auch in dieser Krümmung steckt eine gewisse Anmut und Schönheit, nicht Unterwerfung an eine unliebsame Macht, sondern Hingabe an die Reize der Natur.

Die Küsten - 365 Strände und Buchten - sind der Anfang zu einem kleinen Stückchen Paradies; das gleiche Paradies, das Christopher Columbus im Jahre 1493 hier antraf, als er auf seiner zweiten Reise in seine 'Neue Welt' diese Inseln entdeckte und ihnen die Namen 'Antigua' und 'Barbuda' gab.

# Geographie und Frühgeschichte

Die Insel Antigua ist etwa 280 Quadratkilometer, Barbuda etwa 160 Quadratkilometer groß. Gemeinsam mit der Insel Redonda machen die beiden Inseln den Staat Antigua und Barbuda aus. Redonda ist unbewohnt, auf Antigua leben ca. 70.000 Menschen, auf Barbuda etwa 1.200.

Diese Inseln waren bereits vor der Geburt Christi bewohnt. Man hat herausgefunden, dass bereits 1775 v.Ch. Menschen des Mesoindischen Zeitalters in Jolly Beach auf Antigua lebten. Sie wurden 'Siboney' (Steinmenschen) genannt. Etwa 500 v.Chr. lebten einige Nomadenvölker in North Sound, wo sie vom Fischfang lebten, nach diesen war die Insel jedoch bis 35 n.Chr. unbewohnt. Zu jener Zeit verließen amerikanische Indianer des Arawak-Stammes ihr Zuhause in Venezuela und siedelten sich in der Nähe der Indian Creek an, wo sie Fischerei, etwas Landwirtschaft und Töpferei betrieben. Etwa 1200 n.Chr. kamen die Caribs, ebenfalls amerikanische Indianer, von Südamerika auf die Inselgruppe. Sie errichteten Siedlungen in Dominica und St. Kitts, von denen aus sie die Arawaks auf Antigua überfielen, deren Frauen und Kinder als Sklaven verschleppten und die Männer ermordeten. Sie nannten Antigua 'Waladli', Barbadu 'Waomoni' und Redonda 'Ocanamanru'.

Die meisten Antiguaner und Barbudaner haben die Insel Redonda, die seit jeher als abgelegene, steile und unzugängliche Felseninsel gilt, niemals gesehen. ‹ber die Jahre wurde sie auf verschiedenartigste Weise genutzt. Ein paar Jahre lang wurde auf dem Felssattel Kassawa für die Seefahrer angebaut, dann wurden auf der Insel Briefmarken gedruckt und Phosphate aus Vogelguano abgebaut. Heute ist die Insel jedoch nur noch ein Vogelparadies.

Es gibt allerdings einen Mann, der Redonda als 'sein Königreich' bezeichnet. Der Engländer Jon M. Wynne Tyson aus Sussex behauptet, König der Vulkanfelseninsel zu sein, wo seine einzigen Untertanen Vögel sind, die, vom Flug ermüdet, hier hauptsächlich zum Verrichten ihrer Notdurft landen, ehe sie sich zuträglicheren Orten zuwenden. Tysons Besitzanspruch geht auf das Jahr 1865 zurück, als der Engländer Matthew Dowdy Shiell während einer Segelreise nach Redonda gelangte und mit dem Stolz eines gerade gewordenen Vaters die Insel zum Königreich für seinen Sohn erklärte. Wie es sich gehört, wurde der Sohn auf die Insel gebracht und offiziell zum König Philippe I. gekrönt. Nach seinem Tode wurde der Thron an den Dichter John Gawsworth vermacht, der eine Reihe bekannter Schriftsteller, wie Dylan Thomas, Ellery Queen, J.B. Priestley und Lawrence Dureel mit verschiedenen Positionen am Hofe betraute. Gawsworth wurde König Juan I, nach ihm ging das Königreich an Wynne Tyson, der sich zu King Juan II ernannte. Allerdings hat keine Regierung von Antigua und Barbuda das 'Königreich' bislang ernst genommen.

# Ein kurzer Abriss der neueren Geschichte

Antigua wurde von den Europäern zum ersten Mal im Jahre 1632 besiedelt, als die Engländer von ihrer westindischen Hauptkolonie St. Kitts aus einen Trupp Männer, angeführt von Captain Edward Warner, zu der Insel absandte, um diese in Besitz zu nehmen. Abgesehen von einer kurzen Zeit im Jahre 1666, als die Insel von den Franzosen erobert wurde, blieb sie in britischem Besitz bis zu ihrer Unabhängigkeit am 1. November 1981. Auch heute noch ist das Land ein monarchischer Staat, dessen Oberhaupt die britische Königin Elizabeth II ist. Barbuda war zunächst ein separater britischer Besitz, wurde aber am 1. August 1860 offiziell an Antigua angegliedert.

Der Mann, der die Verbindung zwischen Antigua und Barbados schuf, war Sir Christopher Codrington, der im Jahre 1674 von Barbados nach Antigua kam und dort die erste große Zuckerplantage anlegte, die er nach dem Namen seiner Tochter Betty's Hope benannte. Zucker dominierte Antigua bis in die 1970er Jahre. Das meiste Land wurde für den Zuckeranbau verwendet, wodurch auf Jahre hin schwere wirtschaftliche Probleme hinterlassen wurden. Codrington pachtete außerdem die Insel Barbuda von der Britischen Krone für die jährliche Pachtsumme von einer fetten Sau - falls angefordert. Es wurde behauptet, dass Barbuda eine 'Zuchtfarm' war, auf der Codrington 'Qualitätssklaven' züchtete, wobei es allerdings bis heute keine echten Beweise für diese Behauptungen gibt.

Codringtons erfolgreiche Zuckerplantage zog auch weitere Plantagenbetreiber an und schon bald breiteten sich die Zuckerplantagen über ganz Antigua aus. Im gleichen Maße, wie der Zuckeranbau wuchs, wurde die einheimische Vegetation immer mehr ausgerottet. Gregson Davis schreibt dazu in 'Antigua Black': "Die immergrünen Wälder wurden genauso gründlich wie unwiederbringlich und kurzsichtig eingeebnet." Heute gibt es, abgesehen von dem üppigen Fig Tree Drive, bedauerlich wenig Wälder und Gehölz auf Antigua. Die Verunstaltung der natürlichen Schönheit der Insel ist jedoch nicht die einzige Auswirkung der mutwilligen Zerstörung: da die Bäume fehlten, blieb auch der Regen aus und Dürre machte sich breit. Die Regierung hat versucht, dieses Problem durch den Bau des Potswork Dam, einem riesigen, künstlich angelegten See in der Mitte von Antigua anzugehen und hat außerdem eine Entsalzungsanlange gebaut, um Meerwasser für den Haus- und industriellen Gebrauch nutzbar zu machen.

Im Jahre 1678 bestand die Hälfte der Inselbevölkerung aus Sklaven, die von der Westküste Afrikas hierher verschleppt waren und auf den Zuckerplantagen arbeiteten. Die Freilassung der Sklaven Antiguas erfolgte 1. August 1834, am gleichen Tag, an dem auch die Sklaven auf den Bahamas und auf Bermuda freigelassen wurden. Die anderen britischen Kolonien in der Karibik richteten jedoch zunächst eine vierjährige ‹bergangsphase ein, "Lehrzeit" genannt, bevor sie den Sklaven totale Freiheit gewährten. Der Grund für die sofortige Freilassung der antiguanischen Sklaven war rein wirtschaftlicher Natur: da für die Sklaven die einzige Art des Broterwerbs die Arbeit auf den Zuckerplantagen war, ließen die Plantagenbesitzer sie frei, zahlten ihnen ein lächerliches Gehalt und entzogen sich somit jeglicher Verpflichtung, ihnen Unterkunft, Kleidung oder Nahrung zu geben.

In der Zwischenzeit war Barbuda in Großbritannien so weit in Vergessenheit geraten, dass die Regierungsbeauftragten, die für das Gesetz zur Abschaffung der Sklaverei zuständig waren, die Insel in ihrem Dokument nicht erwähnten. Codrington hielt auch weiterhin Sklaven auf Barbuda, am 2. April 1860 sandte er jedoch ein Schreiben an alle Sklaven, in dem er sie aufforderte, auf seinen Plantagen auf Antigua zu arbeiten, da es auf Barbuda für sie nichts zu tun gäbe. Die Sklaven widersetzten sich. Am 1. August 1860 wurde Barbuda durch einen von Queen Victoria auf der Isle of Wight unterzeichneten Erlass an Antigua angeschlossen. Weder die antiguanische Legislative noch die befreiten Sklaven Barbudas waren glücklich über diese Entwicklung - erstere waren der Ansicht, dass dies eine zusätzliche Belastung ihres Schatzamtes bedeutete, letztere hegten Hass gegenüber Antigua, da die Insel über die Jahre hinweg zu einem Ort der Bestrafung geworden war.

Das Leben der schwarzen Menschen auf Antigua und Barbados wurde nach ihrer Freilassung nicht einfacher. Rechtlich gesehen waren sie zwar frei, aber sie waren immer noch an ihre Plantagen gebunden. Nur ihrer Zähigkeit und ihrem Fleiß ist es zu verdanken, dass sie es, obwohl sie von brutaler Sklaverei in größte Armut gestoßen wurden, in den vier Jahren nach ihrer Freilassung von besitzlosen Lohnarbeitern zu Eigentümern von 1.037 Häusern in 27 Dörfern brachten.

Die Arbeitsbedingungen wurden jedoch immer untragbarer und als Ende der 1930er Jahre die Weltwirtschaft zusammenbrach, war in Antigua, wie auf den übrigen West Indies, die Zeit für ƒnderungen reif geworden. Unter dem Vorsitz von Lord Moyne wurde eine Königliche Kommission in die Region gesandt, die im Dezember 1938 in Antigua eintreffen sollte. Am 1. Januar 1939 hielt Sir Walter Citrine, ein Kommissionsmitglied, eine öffentliche Ansprache im Schulzimmer der anglikanischen Kathedrale in St. John's, der Hauptstadt von Antigua. In seiner Ansprache drang er auf die Gründung von Gewerkschaften, um auf diese Weise für die Rechte der Arbeiter zu kämpfen.

Unter seiner Zuhörerschaft befand sich Vere Conrwall Bird, der ein Jahr später in die Exekutive der am 16. Januar 1939 gegründeten Antigua Trades and Labour Union gewählt wurde. In den darauf folgenden Jahren errang die Gewerkschaft viele Siege bei der Durchsetzung von Rechten und Gerechtigkeit für die Arbeiter. 1943 wurde V.C. Bird zum Gewerkschaftspräsidenten gewählt. Seit dieser Zeit ist der Name Bird zum Synonym für Antigua und Barbuda geworden.

1946 wurde Bird in die Legislative der Gewerkschaft gewählt und erhielt einen Sitz im Exekutivrat. Nach großer Aufruhr seitens der Gewerkschaft wurde für die Regierungswahlen im Jahre 1951 ein allgemeines Stimmrecht für Erwachsene eingeführt. Die Gewerkschaft stellte acht Kandidaten für den Wahlkampf und gewann alle Sitze. 1956 wurde ein ministerielles Regierungssystem eingeführt und auch hier gewann die Gewerkschaft unter der Leitung von V.C. Bird alle Sitze. 1961 wurde die Position eines Obersten Ministers eingeführt und die Anzahl der Sitze in der Legislative von acht auf zehn erhöht. Barbuda, das zuvor zum Wahlkreis St. John's gehörte, wurde ein eigener Wahlkreis, V.C. Bird der erste Oberste Minister.

Im Februar 1967 stellte Antigua einen Antrag auf Unabhängigkeit von Großbritannien, konnte aber nicht mehr als den Status eines 'Associated State' erringen - einem Staat mit Verfügungsgewalt über alle internen Angelegenheiten und einen Teil seiner Außenbeziehungen. Als Antigua und Barbuda am 1. November 1981 volle Unabhängigkeit von Großbritannien erhielten, wurde V.C. Bird der erste Premierminister des Landes.

Zwischen 1967 und 1981 gab es eine Reihe politischer Unruhen auf Antigua und Barbuda, durch welche die Stärke der Antigua Trades and Labour Union (AT&LU) gebrochen wurde. Mitte der 50er bildete sich bei Freiberuflern und Unternehmern Widerstand gegenüber Bird und der Gewerkschaft. Allerdings wurden die von ihnen für die Wahlen der Jahre 1956, 1961 und 1966 aufgestellten Kandidaten jedes Mal geschlagen. 1968 endete jedoch die Solidarität innerhalb der Arbeiterklasse - die bis dahin immer das Rückgrat für Bird und seine Gewerkschaft gewesen war - mit der Gründung der Antigua Workers Union (AWU), einer von unzufriedenen Mitgliedern der AT&LU neu gegründeten Gewerkschaft, die von deren ehemaligem Generalsekretär George Walter geleitet wurde. 1970 wurde eine neue Partei gegründet, die Progressive Labour Movement, mit starker Unterstützung der AWU. Im Jahre 1971 gewann die Partei die Regierungswahlen und Walter wurde neuer Premierminister.

Während der Walter-Regierung erlebte das Land steigende ÷lpreise und einen massiven Anstieg seiner Importkosten, was sich nachteilig auf den Tourismus auswirkte. Die Auswirkungen waren verheerend. Hinzu kam, dass Walters Regierung in einem Versuch, sich V.C. Bird und seiner Antigua Labour Party (ALP) zu entledigen, Gesetze zur Einschränkung der Presse- und Versammlungsfreiheit verabschiedete. Diese Maßnahmen, inmitten einer Wirtschaftskrise, riefen heftige Reaktionen unter den politischen Kräften hervor. Bei den Regierungswahlen 1976 gewannen V.C. Bird und die ALP wieder die Mehrheit, aber zum ersten Male gab es im Parlament eine Opposition.

Die ALP gewann auch die Regierungswahlen im Jahre 1980 und führte Antigua und Barbuda in die Unabhängigkeit, trotz Protesten seitens einiger barbudanischer Führer, die entweder "eigenständige Unabhängigkeit oder weiterhin britische Kolonie" sein wollten.

Bei den Regierungswahlen von 1984 gewann die ALP wieder alle Sitze auf Antigua.

Die zentrale Rolle des Zuckers für die Wirtschaft endete im Jahre 1972, als die Zuckerindustrie stillgelegt wurde und die Touristenzahlen, die 1960 ganz klein angefangen hatten, plötzlich in die Höhe schossen. Seit 1976 haben Antigua und Barbuda eine bemerkenswerte Umwandlung erlebt - die Wirtschaft ist mit jedem Jahr stetig gewachsen, hauptsächlich aufgrund des wachsenden Tourismus und den damit verbundenen Hotels, Restaurants, Boutiquen und Arbeitsplätzen.

Neben dem Bau von Hotels wurden auch große Summen in die touristische Infrastruktur investiert. 1977 kamen 67.412 Touristen per Flugzeug auf die Inseln, im Jahre 1997 hatte sich deren Anzahl verdreifacht. Antigua besitzt einen gut ausgestatteten Flughafen mit Direktverbindungen nach Frankfurt, London, Miami, New York und Toronto. Darüber hinaus ist Antigua das Tor zur östlichen Karibik und Südamerika, mit täglichen Flügen der auf Antigua ansässigen Luftfahrtgesellschaft Leeward Islands Air Transport (LIAT).

Investiert wurde auch in den Tiefseehafen in St. John's. Die modernen Hafenanlagen können neben großen Frachtschiffen auch die dickbäuchigen Passagierschiffe für Kreuzfahrten aufnehmen. 1977 betrug die Zahl der in

Antigua an Land gehenden Kreuzfahrtreisenden 35.795; 1997 war die Zahl auf über 250.000 gestiegen.

Als auf Antigua Zucker angebaut wurde, waren über neunzig Prozent des Landes mit Zuckerrohr bepflanzt, während der Anbau anderer Agrargüter von den Plantagenbesitzern weitgehend verhindert wurde. Heute ist ein sichtbarer Auftrieb in der Agrarwirtschaft ersichtlich, insbesondere was den Anbau von Obst und Gemüse anbelangt. Die *Antigua Black*, eine kleine, süße Ananas und eines der auf dem Landeswappen abgebildeten Symbole, wird heute für den Export angebaut, desgleichen Melonen und verschiedene Gemüsesorten.

Die Wirtschaft des Landes hat außerdem von einem guten Investitionsklima profitiert. Antigua und Babuda besitzen zollfreien Zugang zu den Märkten der

karibischen Commonwealth-Länder, zu Kanada, den Vereinigten Staaten und der Europäischen Union. Herstellungsbetriebe, insbesondere in die USA und Kanada exportierende Randindustrien, haben auf Antigua ein freundliches und hilfsbereites Arbeitsklima gefunden, wozu auch Steuervergünstigen gehören, steuerfreie Urlaubsreisen sowie ausgebildete und tüchtige Arbeitskräfte. Heute werden auf den Inseln Bekleidung, Betten und Matratzen, Farbe, Elektrogeräte und Möbel gefertigt.

Diese Entwicklungen haben dazu geführt, dass es für die Antiguaner und Barbudaner mehr und bessere Arbeitsplätze in den Bereichen Tourismus, Landwirtschaft und Industrie gibt. Mit dem Ergebnis, dass der Lebensstandard unter den Einheimischen heute ein besserer ist als jemals zuvor in der Geschichte des Landes.

# Von früh bis spät

Vom ersten Morgengrauen an macht sich die Sonne in jedem Winkel der Häuser und Hotels bemerkbar und treibt den Schlaf aus den Gesichtern.

Die Bauern in den ländlichen Gegenden Antiguas stehen allerdings schon vor Sonnenaufgang auf und bereiten sich eine Mahlzeit zu, ehe sie sich auf den Weg zu ihren Ländereien machen.

Viele dieser Bauern besitzen kleine Anwesen, gerade genug, um ihren Lebensunterhalt zu bestreiten. Jahr für Jahr produzieren sie landwirtschaftliche Erzeugnisse zum Verkauf auf dem Markt oder an die Government Marketing Corporation. Viele dieser Bauern sind ältere Menschen, die ihr Leben lang hart gearbeitet haben, damit ihre Kinder eine Ausbildung erhalten - mit dem Ergebnis, dass sie die meisten ihrer Kinder an die Büros und Hotels verloren haben. Auch die jüngeren Menschen stehen schon vor Sonnenaufgang auf, um mit den Bussen vom Land nach St. John's zu fahren.

Einen Morgen, um im Bett zu bleiben, gibt es nicht - auch nicht für die Urlauber. Der größte Luxus ist es, sich am Strand zu aalen und sich den gegensätzlichen Empfindungen der wärmenden Sonne und der kühlen Brise hinzugeben. Zunächst gibt es jedoch Frühstück in jeglicher Form - amerikanisch, europäisch und westindisch. Und welch' köstliche Früchte es gibt: Ananas, Papau und Guajave, die bereits vor Kolumbus' Zeiten hier wuchsen; Bananen und Orangen, die von den Spaniern in die Karibik gebracht wurden, außerdem Mango, von den Briten aus Westafrika hierher gebracht. Der größte Luxus ist es, mit dem Ozean im Hintergrund zu frühstücken und zuzuhören, wie die Wellen sanft auf die Küste zurollen und über den festen Sand schwappen.

Das Angebot an Wassersportvergnügungen zeigt sich als eine farbenfrohe Mischung aus Jetskis, Katamaranen, Jachten und geblähten Segeln. Daneben Verkäufer - zumeist Frauen - die farbenfrohe Kleider, T-Shirts, Perlen und aus einheimischen Materialien hergestellten Schmuck verkaufen.

Die Strandbar öffnet früh und betreibt einen regen Verkauf an Fruchtpunsch für die Kinder und an Rumpunschgetränken.

Das Meer bietet seine eigenen Attraktionen, die sich am besten durch Schnorcheln oder Sporttauchen erkunden lassen. Das Wasser über den Riffs ist kristallklar und birgt ein farbenfrohes Meeresleben mit in alle Richtungen flitzenden Papageifischen, Kugelfischen, Muränen und Schnepfenfischen. Passionierte Angler finden ein reiches und vielfältiges Angebot an Schnappern, Zackenbarschen, Wahoos, Königsfischen und Hummern, die hier in den Gewässern um Antigua und Barbuda beheimatet sind.

Die Gewässer von Antigua sind außerdem einmal im Jahr Schauplatz für die *Sailing Week*, einem der beliebtesten

Ereignisse im Kalender eines jeden Sportseglers. In dieser Woche gehört es einfach dazu, in irgendeiner Form an einem der fünf strapaziösen Rennen teilzunehmen, die jeweils in der letzten Aprilwoche stattfinden. Für die im Jahre 1964 für einheimische Segler ins Leben gerufenen Veranstaltung spendete die British Overseas Airways Corporation (BOAC, heute British Airways) einen Silberpokal für den Gewinner der Segelregatta zwischen Guadeloupe und Antigua. Die Organisatoren, ermutigt durch diese Anerkennung, beschlossen im Jahre 1967, eine dreitägige Regattaveranstaltung daraus zu machen. Seither gibt es für die *Sailing Week* kein Zurück mehr.

Bei den Regatten geht es vor allem um Geschicklichkeit und Ausdauer. Hunderte von Besuchern reisen alljährlich nach Antigua, um der Veranstaltung beizuwohnen, desgleichen Tausende von Einwohnern, die sich Aussichtspunkte an der Küste entlang sichern, um zu verfolgen, wie Weltmeisterschaftsjachten Rumpf an Rumpf mit weniger bekannten, aber deswegen nicht weniger ehrgeizigen Seglern durch die Gewässer kreuzen. Und während die *Sailing Week* ausgezeichnete Unterhaltung auf dem Meere bietet, ist sie außerdem eine hervorragende Gelegenheit für Festlichkeiten an der Küste. Segler und Zuschauer werden gleichermaßen angezogen von den vielen Strandpartys, bei denen der Alkohol fließt und Musik und gute Laune jedermann zusammenbringen.

Im Zentrum all dieser Aktivitäten steht *Nelson's Dockyard* in English Harbour, benannt nach dem englischen Admiral Horatio Nelson. Nelson kam 1784 im Alter von 26 Jahren nach Antigua, wo er drei Jahre lang blieb. Das Haus, in dem er damals wohnte, ist heute ein Museum.

English Harbour war jedoch schon vor Nelsons Zeiten ein wichtiger Ort. Anfang 1700 wurde es zusammen mit Port Royal in Jamaica zu einer der permanenten Marinestationen in der Karibik gemacht. Das auf einem alten Vulkankegel gelegene English Harbour besteht aus mehr oder weniger vom Land völlig eingeschlossenen Hafenbecken, die nur über eine enge Passage vom Meer aus zu erreichen sind - auf diese Weise war der Hafen nicht nur gegen Unwetter, sondern auch gegen Einblicke vom Meer geschützt.

Zur Verteidigung dieses von der Natur vorgegebenen, strategischen Ortes wurden zwischen 1780 und 1790 auf den überhängenden Bergrücken Befestigungen gebaut, und zwar auf Befehl von General Thomas Shirley, dem General und Obersten Gouverneur der Leeward Islands. Die Ruinen dieser Militärfestungen auf den so genannten *Shirley Heights* stehen auch heute noch. Ebenfalls dort befindet sich *Clarence House*, in dem der englische Duke of Clarence und spätere König William IV wohnte, während er in der Königlichen Marine diente.

Ein Besuch St. John's, der Hauptstadt von Antigua, darf auf keinen Fall fehlen. Obwohl die Stadt überfüllt ist mit Menschen und Verkehr, geht das Leben entspannt und gelassen einher. Die Geschäfte sind zum Bersten mit Waren gefüllt, hin und wieder wird der Verkehrs- und Menschenlärm von Musikrhythmen unterbrochen, die sich aus einem Gebäude oder Musikshop auf die Straßen ergießen, wenn etwa eine Band in einem der Geschäfte oder Gebäude probt.

Die Stadt wurde um eine Festung herum errichtet, deren Bau im Jahre 1672 auf Rat Island begann. 1683 wurde die erste St. John's-Kirche gebaut und die sich hier ansiedelnde Gemeinde gewann schon bald an Größe. 1702 wurde ein Markt errichtet und ein kreuzweges Straßennetz errichtet. Als Nächstes wurden die Verwaltungsgebäude gebaut: Government House im Jahre 1801 und ein Hauptpostamt im Jahre 1850. In der Mitte des 19. Jahrhunderts erlebte St. John's

einen Bauboom, nachdem viele Gebäude in einem Brand im Jahre 1841 zerstört worden waren. Die verschiedenen Bauphasen haben in der Stadt eine Mischung architektonischer Stile hinterlassen: georgianisch, viktorianisch, romantisch und international. Bei dem jüngsten Sanierungsprojekt wurden verfallene Häuser durch Gebäude ersetzt, die an die architektonische Form aus der Mitte des 19. Jahrhunderts erinnern. Die Vielfalt unterschiedlicher Strukturen fällt ebenso ins Auge wie die Bedeutung der einzelnen Gebäude, in denen sich Vergangenheit und Gegenwart widerspiegeln.

Da Antigua im 18. Und 19. Jahrhundert eine bedeutende Insel für den Zuckeranbau war, ist St. John's schon immer eine geschäftige Handelsstadt gewesen. Berichten zufolge lagen Mitte des 19. Jahrhunderts zu jeder Zeit mindestens zwölf Schiffe aus London oder Liverpool im Hafen. Die Stadt ist ein lebhaftes Handelszentrum geblieben und die Heimat einer Reihe von Banken, von denen viele Zweigstellen internationaler Banken sind.

Darüber hinaus bietet St. John's Restaurants, Geschäfte und einige historisch bedeutende Stätten. *The Old Court House* beherbergt heute ein Museum und Archive, welche eine Fundgrube für historische Dokumente und ein Schaukasten für die Geschichte des Landes sind. Das Gebäude wurde zum ersten Mal im Jahre 1747 errichtet, wurde aber 1843 in einem Erdbeben zerstört und anschließend wieder aufgebaut. Ein weiteres Erdbeben im Jahre 1947 beschädigte es erneut, so dass es ein zweites Mal restauriert werden musste. Ganz in der Nähe befindet sich *St. John's Cathedral*, am gleichen Orte wie die ursprüngliche Kirche aus dem Jahre 1683, und nach wie vor wird die Silhouette von den beiden Kirchtürmen im Barockstil dominiert.

Nicht weit davon entfernt befindet sich

auch Antiguas Freizeitgelände - ein Veranstaltungsort für viele karibische und internationale Cricket- und Fußballspiele. An der Stelle, an dem sich heute das Freizeitgelände befindet, wurde im Jahre 1736 Antiguas Nationalheld, ein Sklave namens Prince Klaass gefoltert und umgebracht, nachdem er eine Rebellion zur Befreiung seines Volkes angestiftet hatte. Der gleiche Geist, der damals nach Freiheit strebte, lebt auch heute noch weiter und findet seinen Ausdruck im Karneval. Der Karneval findet alljährlich während der letzten Juli- und der ersten Augustwoche statt, zum Jahrestag der Abschaffung der Sklaverei am 1. August 1834. Bezeichnenderweise finden die Karnevalsveranstaltungen, bei denen sich der schöpferische Geist der Antiguaner in ungeahnte Höhen schwingt, auf dem gleichen Grund und Boden statt, auf dem die Plantagenbesitzer den Geist der Freiheit zu erdrosseln versuchten, der in der Person von Prince Klaass lebte.

Wenn die Sonne endlich untergeht und wieder einen Tag seinem Ende und der Nacht entgegenbringt, kommen die Jachten zum Anlegen zurück; die Strände leeren sich, während sich die Urlauber den Restaurants und Nightclubs zuwenden und die Büros und Fabriken die Menschen zu ihren abendlichen Unternehmungen entlassen. Eine kühle Luft steigt über den Inseln herab, während die Sonne hinter dem Horizont verschwindet. Jetzt ist es der Mond, der die Herrschaft übernimmt und ein romantisches Licht über das Land und die Gewässer von Karibik und Atlantik wirft.

Der Tag war voller Unternehmungen, die Nacht hat ihn sanft zur Ruhe gebracht und es wurde ein Stück vom Glanz des "kleinen Stückchen Paradieses" festgehalten - Antigua und Barbuda.

# Le jour se lève

Le soleil, tel une énorme orange mûre, se lève lentement sur la mer des Caraïbes. Des rais de lumière, certains jaunes, d'autres rouges, d'autres encore d'un blanc lumineux, voguent à la surface de l'eau, dansant au sommet de petites vagues légères courant vers un rivage encore blotti dans l'ombre fuyante de la nuit, mais laissant déjà deviner des plages de sable blanc et doré. Le jour se lève sur Antigua et Barbuda... où chaque jour c'est l'été.

À mesure que le soleil s'élève dans le ciel, sa lueur dorée disparaît, cédant à une éblouissante luminosité qui s'avance sur la mer et sur la terre. L'air est encore frais, car si le soleil a commencé à proclamer son empire sur la terre, sa chaleur encore faible ne parvient pas à pénétrer l'alizé du nord-est, dont le souffle puissant et régulier parcourt la mer.

Dans une tradition séculaire, de minuscules bateaux de pêche oscillent sur la mer, retournant vers le rivage chargés de poissons pour le marché du matin. Les pêcheurs sont sortis cette nuit sachant que les premières lueurs du jour attireraient les poissons à la surface de l'eau, dans un rituel de bienvenue au rayonnement du soleil naissant, avant que sa chaleur ne les force à rechercher des eaux plus fraîches au fond de l'océan. Le souffle cadencé des petits hors-bord des bateaux de pêche se mêle au grondement plus fort des moteurs des scooters des mers, des canots automobiles et des yachts, tandis que ceux qui s'occupent des visiteurs impatients de profiter au maximum de leur séjour aux Caraïbes commencent à préparer leur équipement pour la journée.

Petit à petit, les gens font leur apparition: ce sont tout d'abord de jeunes autochtones d'Antigua et Barbuda qui courent sur la plage et à l'occasion plongent dans l'eau pour se revigorer dans sa vivifiante fraîcheur. Les visiteurs paraissent eux aussi dans la lumière du petit matin et, dans un sentiment d'attente enfin satisfaite, plongent dans la mer, étirant le dos, détendant les muscles, laissant les tensions s'évanouir, le visage levé pour sentir les rayons glorieux du soleil leur picoter la peau.

Les oiseaux aussi prennent part à l'activité matinale. Il existe 140 espèces d'oiseaux à Antigua et Barbuda, dont 90 sont vues régulièrement. Certains sont des chasseurs. C'est le cas du pélican brun, que l'on voit frôler la surface de l'eau et soudain plonger dans la mer pour en émerger tout aussi soudainement, son repas du matin serré dans son bec. D'autres volent d'arbre en arbre, s'interpellant de leur chant et ajoutant à ce sentiment d'une nature dans toute sa perfection. Le "bananaquit" et le petit bouvreuil des Antilles, noir ou gris, la gorge tachée de rouge, sont les plus communs.

Alors que le soleil poursuit son ascension, baignant la terre de lumière, les couleurs prennent vie. Les feuilles sont maintenant d'un vert vif, les fleurs - le

bougainvillier, l'hibiscus et le laurier-rose - sont rouges, jaunes, blanches et pourpre. Les cocotiers et autres palmiers, qui ornent majestueusement les rivages de ces îles depuis des décennies, se dressent vers un ciel bleu clair, ponctué de doux nuages blancs. Ça et là, on voit un palmier, soit très vieux soit très jeune, que la pression du vent a plié. Mais même cette courbe possède une certaine grâce, une élégance qui évoque non pas la soumission à une force redoutée, mais la capitulation devant le charme de la nature.

Les rivages - 365 plages et criques - sont le début d'un petit coin de paradis; le même paradis que celui découvert par Christophe Colomb en 1493, lorsqu'au cours de son deuxième voyage vers ce qu'il appela le "Nouveau Monde", il vit ces îles et les nomma "Antigua" et "Barbuda".

# La géographie et la préhistoire

Antigua s'étend sur 280 kilomètres carrés et Barbuda sur 160 kilomètres carrés. Les deux îles forment, avec l'île de Redonda, le territoire d'Antigua et Barbuda. Redonda est inhabitée. Antigua compte environ 70 000 habitants et Barbuda environ 1 200.

Ces îles furent habitées avant la naissance du Christ ; il a en effet été établi qu'un peuple de l'âge méso-indien vivait à Antigua dès 1775 av. J.-C., à Jolly Beach. Ce peuple fut appelé "Siboney" (peuple de la pierre). Même si des nomades ont vécu et péché à North Sound vers l'an 500 av. J.-C., l'île n'a pas été colonisée avant 35 ap. J.-C., lorsque des Amérindiens de la tribu Arawak quittèrent leur Venezuela natal pour s'établir près d'Indian Creek où ils créèrent des villages de pêche et se lancèrent dans l'agriculture et la poterie. Vers 1200 ap. J.-C., une autre tribu d'Amérindiens, les Caribs, remonta également la chaîne d'îles depuis l'Amérique du Sud. Elle s'établit à la Dominique et à Saint-Christophe, d'où elle attaqua les Arawaks d'Antigua, prenant femmes et enfants pour esclaves et tuant les hommes. Elle appela Antigua "Waladli", Barbuda "Wa'omoni" et Redonda "Ocanamanru".

La grande majorité des habitants d'Antigua et de Barbuda n'a jamais vu Redonda, qui a toujours été considérée comme une "île rocheuse isolée, escarpée et menaçante". Au fil des ans, elle a été utilisée de diverses façons, mais jamais pour très longtemps. On y a par exemple cultivé le manioc pour les marins sur le col du roc, émis des timbres-poste et produit du phosphate à partir du guano d'oiseaux. Mais c'est seulement en tant qu'abri pour les oiseaux qu'elle reste utile.

Il est cependant un homme qui considère Redonda comme son "royaume". Jon M. Wynne Tyson, originaire du Sussex, en Angleterre, déclare être le roi de ce roc volcanique où ses seuls sujets sont les oiseaux qui, fatigués de voler, se posent pour faire leurs ablutions avant de repartir pour des endroits plus favorables. Les prétentions de Tyson remontent à 1865 lorsque Matthew Dowdy Shiell, naviguant aux abords de Redonda et rempli de la fierté que lui donnait son récent statut de père, décréta qu'il s'agissait du royaume de son fils. Le garçon fut bien entendu emmené sur l'île et officiellement proclamé roi Phillipe I$^{er}$. À sa mort, le trône fut légué au poète John Gawsworth qui nomma plusieurs écrivains éminents, tels que Dylan Thomas, Ellery Queen, J. B. Priestly et Lawrence Durrell, à différentes fonctions royales. Gasworth devint le roi Juan I$^{er}$ en transmettant la couronne à Wynne Tyson qui se déclara lui-même roi Juan II. Aucun gouvernement d'Antigua et Barbuda n'a encore pris le "royaume" au sérieux.

# Une histoire contemporaine courte

C'est en 1632 qu'Antigua fut pour la première fois colonisée par des Européens, lorsque les Anglais chargèrent un groupe d'hommes de leur principale colonie des Indes occidentales, Saint-Christophe, dirigé par le capitaine Edward Warner, d'en prendre possession. En dehors d'une brève période en 1666 où elle fut prise par les Français, Antigua est restée britannique jusqu'à son indépendance, proclamée le 1$^{er}$ novembre 1981. Aujourd'hui, le pays est toujours un …tat monarchique, dont le chef est Elizabeth II, reine d'Angleterre. Barbuda, possession britannique distincte, fut officiellement annexée à Antigua le 1$^{er}$ août 1860.

Celui qui fut directement responsable du lien entre Antigua et Barbuda est Sir Christopher Codrington. De la Barbade, il vint à Antigua en 1674 où il créa la première grande plantation de canne à sucre, qu'il appela Betty's Hope en souvenir de sa fille. La production de sucre a dominé à Antigua jusqu'aux années 1970, utilisant l'essentiel de la terre et laissant en héritage des problèmes économiques graves. Mais Codrington avait également obtenu de la Couronne britannique le droit de louer Barbuda au prix annuel d'"un cochon gras, si on le demande". Il a été suggéré que Barbuda aurait été un "haras" dans lequel Codrington élevait des "esclaves de qualité". Aucune preuve concrète ne le confirme cependant.

La réussite que la canne à sucre valut à Codrington encouragea d'autres planteurs et, très vite, les plantations de canne à sucre proliférèrent à Antigua. La multiplication des plantations fut accompagnée de la destruction quasi complète de la végétation. Comme Gregson Davis l'indique dans "Antigua Black", "les bois verts furent rasés d'une façon aussi systématique qu'irréversible et à courte vue". D'où, en dehors du luxuriant Fig Tree Drive, l'absence regrettable de forêts et de bois à Antigua aujourd'hui. Mais la mutilation de la beauté naturelle de l'île n'est pas la seule conséquence de la destruction absurde de la végétation : la sécheresse est le principal résultat de l'absence d'arbres pour attirer la pluie. Le gouvernement a cherché à remédier à ce problème en créant le réservoir Potswork Dam, immense lac artificiel au centre d'Antigua, et en construisant une usine de dessalement pour permettre l'utilisation domestique et industrielle de l'eau de mer.

En 1678, la moitié de la population de l'île se composait d'esclaves emmenés de la côte occidentale de l'Afrique pour cultiver la canne à sucre.

L'émancipation des esclaves d'Antigua fut proclamée le 1$^{er}$ août 1834, en même temps que celle des esclaves des Bahamas et des Bermudes. Dans toutes les autres colonies britanniques des Caraïbes, une période de transition de quatre ans appelée "apprentissage" était prévue avant l'octroi de la liberté totale. L'émancipation immédiate des esclaves d'Antigua s'explique par des motifs purement économiques. Comme les esclaves n'avaient pas les moyens de gagner leur vie autrement qu'en travaillant dans les plantations de canne à sucre, les planteurs les libérèrent, leur payèrent un salaire dérisoire et n'eurent dès lors plus à les loger, à les nourrir et à les habiller.

Dans le même temps, la Grande-Bretagne se souvenait si peu de Barbuda que les rédacteurs du projet de loi sur l'abolition de l'esclavage omirent de la mentionner dans le document. Codrington continua à maintenir les anciens esclaves à Barbuda mais, le 2 avril 1860, écrivit une lettre adressée à tous les esclaves leur proposant d'aller travailler dans ses plantations d'Antigua parce qu'ils n'avaient rien à faire à Barbuda. Ils refusèrent. Le 1er août 1860, sur ordre du Conseil signé par le monarque britannique à l'île de Wight, Barbuda fut annexée à Antigua. Ni le corps législatif d'Antigua ni les esclaves libérés de Barbuda ne se réjouirent du changement - celui-là parce qu'il pressentait que cela pèserait sur ses finances et ceux-ci parce qu'ils n'aimaient pas Antigua qui, au fil des ans, était devenu un lieu de punition.

La condition des noirs d'Antigua et de Barbuda ne fut pas plus facile après l'émancipation. Ils étaient juridiquement libres, mais restaient toujours liés aux plantations.

Que ces salariés sans terre devinrent propriétaires de 1 037 maisons dans 27 villages dans les quatre ans suivant l'émancipation, malgré la brutalité de l'esclavage dont ils venaient de sortir et du dénuement dans lequel ils étaient laissés, témoigne de leur ténacité et de leur ardeur.

Cependant, les conditions devinrent de plus en plus intolérables pour les travailleurs et, à la fin des années 1930, lorsque l'économie s'effondra, Antigua était, comme le reste des Indes occidentales, prête pour le changement. Une commission royale, présidée par Lord Moyne, fut envoyée dans la région et arriva à Antigua en décembre 1938. Le 1er janvier 1939, un membre de la commission, Sir Walter Citrine, pris la parole lors d'une réunion publique organisée dans la salle de classe de la cathédrale anglicane de Saint John's, capitale d'Antigua. Il appela à la formation de syndicats pour lutter pour les droits des travailleurs.

Dans l'audience se trouvait Vere Cornwall Bird, qui fut élu membre du bureau d'Antigua Trades and Labour Union, le syndicat d'Antigua formé le 16 janvier 1939. Au cours des années qui suivirent, le syndicat remporta de nombreuses victoires allant dans le sens de la justice et des droits des travailleurs. En 1943, V. C. Bird fut élu président du syndicat.

Le nom de Bird est depuis lors synonyme d'Antigua et Barbuda.

Bird fut élu membre du corps législatif en 1946 et obtint un siège au Conseil de direction. En 1951, après beaucoup d'agitation au sein du syndicat, le suffrage universel des adultes fut introduit pour les élections générales. Le syndicat sélectionna huit candidats aux élections et remporta tous les sièges. En 1956, un système de gouvernement ministériel fut introduit et, une fois de plus, le syndicat, présidé par V. C. Bird, remporta tous les sièges du corps législatif. En 1961, le poste de ministre "principal" fut créé et le nombre de sièges passa de huit à dix au corps législatif, Barbuda devenant une circonscription électorale à part entière après avoir été attachée à Saint John's. V. C. Bird fut le premier ministre "principal" du pays.

En février 1967, Antigua demanda son indépendance à la Grande-Bretagne mais n'obtint que le statut d'"...tat associé", "responsable de ses affaires intérieures et d'une partie de ses relations extérieures". V. C. devint le premier Premier ministre. Le 1er novembre 1981, lorsqu'Antigua et Barbuda obtint de la Grande-Bretagne son indépendance totale, Bird devint également le premier Premier ministre du pays.

Cependant, entre 1967 et 1981, Antigua et Barbuda traversa une période de troubles politiques qui mit fin à l'emprise d'Antigua Trades and Labour Union (AT&LU). Au milieu des années 1950, une opposition à Bird et au syndicat s'était formée au sein des professions libérales et du monde des affaires, lesquels présentèrent leurs candidats aux élections de 1956, 1961 et 1966. Tous échouèrent. Cependant, en 1968, la solidarité qui existait au sein de la classe ouvrière et qui était le pivot de la force de Bird prit fin avec la création, par des membres insatisfaits d'AT&LU, du syndicat Antigua Workers Union (AWU), présidé par l'ancien secrétaire général d'AT&LU, George Walter. En 1970, un nouveau parti politique, le Mouvement travailliste progressiste, fut créé avec le soutien marqué de l'AWU. Il remporta les élections générales de 1971. Walter devint Premier ministre.

Le gouvernement de Walter coïncida avec l'augmentation du prix du pétrole, laquelle se répercuta sur le tourisme et augmenta de façon vertigineuse la facture importations du pays. L'effet fut dévastateur. En outre, dans une tentative en vue d'éliminer V. C. Bird et son Antigua Labour Party (ALP), le gouvernement de Walter adopta des lois restrictives limitant la liberté de la presse et de l'assemblée publique. Ces décisions, en pleine crise économique, provoquèrent une réaction violente des forces politiques existantes. Les élections de 1976 ramenèrent V. C. Bird et l'ALP au pouvoir mais avec, pour la première fois, une opposition au Parlement.

L'ALP remporta de nouveau les élections générales de 1980 et obtint l'indépendance d'Antigua et Barbuda malgré les protestations d'un certain nombre de dirigeants de Barbuda qui voulaient "soit l'indépendance séparée, soit rester une colonie britannique".

L'ALP remporta de nouveau tous les sièges d'Antigua lors des élections générales de 1984.

Le sucre perdit la place centrale qu'il occupait jusqu'alors dans l'économie en 1972, lorsque l'industrie fut fermée et que le tourisme, qui avait fait une timide apparition en 1960, arriva en masse. Depuis 1976, Antigua et Barbuda s'est transformée de façon visible : l'économie enregistre chaque année une croissance régulière, grâce au tourisme principalement, qui a amené la construction ou l'agrandissement d'hôtels, l'ouverture de restaurants, de boutiques et la création d'emplois.

En plus des hôtels, d'importants investissements ont été consacrés au maintien des infrastructures touristiques. En 1977, 67 412 touristes sont arrivés par avion. En 1997, ce chiffre avait plus que triplé. Antigua possède un aéroport bien équipé, avec des vols directs pour Francfort, Londres, Miami, New York et Toronto. Antigua constitue également une porte vers les Caraïbes orientales et l'Amérique du Sud, avec des vols quotidiens assurés par la flotte de Leeward Islands Air Transport (LIAT), basée à Antigua.

Le port en eau profonde de Saint John's a également bénéficié des investissements. Les installations modernes du port peuvent accueillir sans difficulté d'énormes cargos ainsi que de grands bateaux de croisière. En 1977, 35 795 passagers de bateaux de croisière avaient débarqué à Antigua ; en 1997, ils étaient plus de 250 000.

Lorsque la canne à sucre a été plantée à Antigua, les champs occupaient plus de quatre-vingt dix pour cent des terres et les planteurs découragèrent les autres cultures. Aujourd'hui cependant, la production agricole bénéficie d'un dynamisme évident, les fruits et les légumes surtout. L'*Antigua Black*, ananas petit mais sucré qui est un des symboles du pays et est représenté sur son blason, est maintenant exporté, ainsi que le melon et divers autres légumes.

L'économie du pays bénéficie également d'un climat favorable en matière d'investissements. Antigua et Barbuda accède en franchise de douane aux marchés des pays caraïbes du Commonwealth, du Canada, des …tats-Unis et des pays de l'Union européenne.

Les entreprises manufacturières, notamment les industries non diversifiées exportant vers les marchés du Canada et des …tats-Unis, ont trouvé un environnement accueillant et efficace, dont

des concessions en franchise de douane, des vacances hors taxe et une main-d'úuvre formée et compétente. L'industrie produit aujourd'hui vêtements, lits et matelas, peinture, matériel électronique, appareils électroménagers et meubles.

Pour les habitants d'Antigua et Barbuda, ces avancées signifient des emplois plus nombreux et meilleurs dans le tourisme, l'agriculture et l'industrie. Les niveaux de vie sont donc aujourd'hui plus élevés que jamais dans l'histoire du pays.

# Du matin au soir

Dès l'aube, le soleil toujours présent se glisse dans tous les coins et recoins des maisons et des hôtels ouvrant leurs yeux gonflés de sommeil.

Mais dans les régions rurales d'Antigua, les agriculteurs sont debout avant le soleil pour préparer leur repas avant d'aller aux champs.

Beaucoup d'entre eux n'ont qu'une petite parcelle de terre dont ils tirent, d'année en année, les récoltes qu'ils vendent au marché ou à la Corporation commerciale du Gouvernement.

Il s'agit pour l'essentiel des moins jeunes, qui travaillent pour pouvoir offrir une formation à leurs enfants qu'ils voient donc presque tous partir pour les bureaux ou les hôtels. Eux aussi se lèvent avant le soleil pour attraper un des bus qui quittent la campagne tôt le matin et déversent leurs passagers à Saint John's.

Même pour le vacancier, aucun matin ne mérite d'être passé au lit. S'allonger sur la plage, en goûtant aux sensations contrastées de la chaleur du soleil se mêlant à la fraîcheur de la brise, est un plus grand luxe. Mais avant cela, il y a le petit déjeunerÖ toutes sortes de combinaisons sont possibles : petit déjeuner américain, européen ou indien occidental. Avec bien sûr des fruits délicieux : l'ananas, la papaye et la goyave, qui étaient là avant Christophe Colomb, la banane et les

oranges, apportées aux Caraïbes par les Espagnols, la mangue, apportée de l'Afrique occidentale par les Anglais. Le plus grand luxe qui soit dans la vie est de prendre son petit déjeuner face à la mer des Caraïbes, en écoutant les vagues s'avancer vers le rivage et venir mourir doucement sur le sable dur.

Sur la plage, scooters des mers, catamarans, yachts et autres voiles gonflées forment une palette de couleurs étourdissante. Il y a aussi les marchands, des femmes pour la plupart, qui vendent robes, t-shirts, perles et bijoux de couleurs fabriqués avec des matières locales.

Le bar de la plage, où se préparent activement les punchs au rhum - au fruit pour les enfants - ouvre tôt.

La mer possède des attraits caractéristiques que la randonnée palmée et la plongée sous-marine permettront mieux d'apprécier. Au-dessus des récifs, l'eau est claire comme le jour et révèle une vie marine très colorée : poissons-perroquets, poissons-globes, murènes et bécasses de mer filant de ci, de là. Les passionnés de pêche trouveront également une variété de poissons comme les vivaneaux, les mérous, les wahoos, les ombrines royales et les homards, qui abondent aux abords d'Antigua et de Barbuda.

C'est dans les eaux d'Antigua que se déroule chaque année la *Semaine de la navigation,* un des événements les plus populaires du calendrier des courses de yachts. Et, cette semaine-là, aucune journée ne sera complète sans la participation, sous une forme ou sous une autre, aux cinq courses éreintantes organisées durant la dernière semaine d'avril. Au départ, il s'agissait d'un divertissement organisé pour les plaisanciers, mais, en 1964, la British Overseas Airways Corporation (BOAC, aujourd'hui British Airways) remit une coupe en argent au vainqueur de la course entre la Guadeloupe et Antigua. Encouragés par cette reconnaissance, les organisateurs décidèrent en 1967 de prévoir trois journées de course. La popularité de la *Semaine de la navigation* ne s'est pas démentie depuis.

Les courses sont une épreuve technique et d'endurance avidement suivie par des centaines de visiteurs, qui arrivent maintenant en masse à Antigua pour l'événement, et par des milliers de gens du pays, qui s'emparent des meilleures places sur la côte pour voir des yachts champions du monde frotter leur coque à celle de bateaux moins connus mais tout aussi ambitieux. Si la *Semaine de la navigation* fait le plaisir des uns sur la mer, elle donne aux autres une tout aussi bonne occasion de faire la fête sur la plage. Les réjouissances organisées sur la plage attirent marins et spectateurs dans un mélange d'alcool, de musique et de camaraderie.

Le centre de toute cette activité se trouve à English Harbour, dans le chantier naval *Nelson's Dockyard*, ainsi nommé en souvenir de l'amiral britannique Horatio Nelson. Nelson arriva à Antigua en 1784, âgé de 26 ans, et y resta trois ans. La maison dans laquelle il vécut est maintenant un musée.

Mais l'importance du port English Harbour remonte à avant Nelson. Au début des années 1700, il fut, avec Port Royal, à la Jamaïque, sélectionné comme l'une des bases navales permanentes des Caraïbes. Situé sur le cône d'un vieux volcan, English Harbour est constitué de bassins pratiquement ceints de terre, reliés à la mer par un étroit passage uniquement, ce qui le protégeait du mauvais temps et en même temps l'empêchait d'être vu de la mer.

C'est pour défendre cet endroit naturellement stratégique que des fortifications furent construites sur la crête des montagnes en surplomb, entre 1780 et 1790, sur ordre du général Thomas Shirley quand il devint capitaine général et gouverneur en chef des îles Sous-le-Vent. Les ruines de ces fortifications édifiées sur les hauteurs que l'on appelle aujourd'hui *Shirley Heights* restent visibles encore aujourd'hui. C'est également là que se trouve *Clarence House*, où vécut le duc de Clarence, futur roi William IV, lorsqu'il servait dans la Marine royale.

Aucune journée ne saurait s'achever sans une visite à Saint John's, la capitale. Elle est encombrée, mais la vie y coule dans une atmosphère décontractée, relaxe. Les magasins débordent de stock et le bruit de la circulation et des conversations est entrecoupé des rythmes qui s'échappent d'un magasin de disques ou d'un bâtiment où s'entraîne un groupe.

La ville fut construite autour d'un fort dont la construction commença sur Rat Island en 1672. En 1683, la première église de Saint John's fut construite et très vite la communauté qui vint dans la région s'agrandit. Un marché fut construit en 1702 et des rues transversales furent ajoutées. Les édifices abritant les institutions furent ensuite bâtis : le gouvernement en 1801 et la poste générale en 1850. Le milieu du XIX$^e$ siècle fut une période d'activité de construction intense à Saint John's, un incendie ayant ravagé plusieurs

édifices en 1841. Le résultat de ces différentes périodes de construction explique le mélange de styles architecturaux de la ville, où les styles classique, victorien, romantique et international cohabitent. Le projet de réaménagement de Saint John's a permis de remplacer des quartiers vétustes par des immeubles dont la forme architecturale évoque le milieu du XIX^e siècle. Si prises collectivement ces différentes structures attirent le regard, chacune d'elles n'en est pas moins importante en tant que représentation d'une époque actuelle ou passée.

Parce qu'Antigua était un important centre de production de sucre aux XVIII^e et XIX^e siècles, Saint John's a toujours été une capitale commerciale animée. On dit qu'au milieu du XIX^e siècle il y avait en permanence au moins douze navires en provenance de Londres ou de Liverpool dans le port. La ville est restée un centre commercial grouillant de vie, contenant un certain nombre de banques, dont de nombreuses succursales d'institutions de réputation internationale.

On trouve à Saint John's restaurants, magasins et sites historiques. L'ancien tribunal, *The Old Court House*, abrite maintenant un musée et un centre d'archives où les documents historiques sont conservés et l'histoire du pays exposée. L'édifice, érigé pour la première fois en 1747, fut restauré à la suite d'un tremblement de terre en 1843. Un autre tremblement de terre l'endommagea de nouveau en 1847, et il dut subir une nouvelle réfection. Tout près se trouve *St John's Cathedral*, construite sur l'emplacement de l'église d'origine, datant de 1683. Ses deux tours, de style baroque, se découpent encore sur l'horizon.

Le terrain de jeux d'Antigua, où se déroulent des matchs de football et de cricket internationaux et caraïbes, n'est pas très loin.

Le héros national d'Antigua, un esclave appelé Prince Klaass ayant conspiré au déclenchement d'une rébellion en vue de libérer son peuple, fut torturé et tué en 1736 à l'endroit même où se trouve l'actuel terrain de jeux d'Antigua. L'esprit qui recherchait la liberté vit encore aujourd'hui et s'exprime à l'époque du carnaval.

Le carnaval a toujours lieu durant la dernière semaine de juillet et la première semaine d'août, période anniversaire de l'abolition de l'esclavage, proclamée le 1^er août 1834. Fait significatif, les spectacles du carnaval, dans lesquels l'esprit créatif du peuple d'Antigua jaillit, ont lieu sur le terrain même où les planteurs ont cherché à tuer l'esprit de la liberté qui habitait le corps de Prince Klaass.

Alors que le soleil se couche sur ces îles, menant un autre jour à sa fin et cédant son empire à la nuit, les yachts rentrent au port ; les plages rendent leurs invités aux restaurants et aux discothèques ; les bureaux et les usines libèrent leurs occupants pour d'autres activités nocturnes. À mesure que le soleil disparaît à l'horizon, l'air frais descend sur les îles. C'est maintenant la lune caraïbe qui est maîtresse des lieux, diffusant une lumière romantique sur la terre et sur les eaux de la mer des Caraïbes et de l'océan Atlantique.

La journée, remplie d'activités, s'est achevée avec la tombée de la nuit et chacun a goûté à ce "petit coin de paradis" qu'est Antigua et Barbuda.

ANTIGUA
AND
BARBUDA
A LITTLE BIT OF PARADISE